# Bon Voyage

## Designs for Travel

# Bon Voyage

## Designs for Travel

Deborah Sampson Shinn

J. G. Links

Paul Fussell

Ralph Caplan

Cooper-Hewitt Museum

The Smithsonian Institution's National Museum of Design

New York

**Motorcycles with luggage**
1978
Courtesy Malcolm S. Forbes,
New York

Cooper-Hewitt Museum
The Smithsonian Institution's
National Museum of Design
2 East 91st Street, New York, N.Y. 10128

LC 86 70423
ISBN 0-91053-50-8
Printed in the United States

Edited by Nancy Aakre
Designed by Katy Homans with
Bethany Johns
Typeset by Trufont Typographers
Printed by Mercantile Printing Company, Inc.

**Library of Congress Cataloging
in Publication Data**

Links, J.G.
Bon voyage: designs for travel

Prepared in conjunction with an exhibition
at the Cooper-Hewitt Museum, sponsored by
Louis Vuitton, Inc.

1. Travel.
2. Travel in art.
3. Design.
I. Fussell, Paul, 1924-
II. Caplan, Ralph.
III. Shinn, Deborah.
IV. Cooper-Hewitt Museum.
G151.L56 1986   910'.74'01471   86-6358
ISBN 0-910503-50-8

**Photo Credits**

Beedle & Cooper 28, 42
A. C. Cooper, Christie's 10, 98, 102
Robert Forbes 4
David Heald 40
Helga Photo Studio 75
Scott Hyde 11, 12, 24, 25, 33, 34, 35,
47, 48, 51, 67, 70, 71, 81, 89, 90, 99,
109, 110, 112, 118, 120, 125
Bruce C. Jones 66
Henry E. Peach 57, 58
Lars Rannegårdh 68
SPADEM © 1986 106
Jeff Tinsley, Smithsonian Institution 64
Jim Wickwire 97

Note: All dimensions are in centimeters
and, unless otherwise specified, are
arranged as height by width by depth.

Cover
**Steam engine train**
early 19th century
Moutonnet (lithographer)
Paris, France
Lithograph, 23 × 63
Collection of Louis Vuitton, Paris

Frontispiece
**South Coast, Natal, South Africa**
1949
Constance Stuart Larrabee (b. 1914)
South Africa and the United States
Photograph
Courtesy Constance Stuart Larrabee,
Chestertown, Maryland

# Contents

# Foreword

Travel is one of the inevitabilities of modern life. Whether we travel from home to work, on seasonal vacations, or even between earth and outer space, we all share the traveler's imperative: to move ourselves and whatever we carry efficiently, perhaps even comfortably, from one place to another. In the larger scheme of history, pilgrims, nomads, and emigrants share aspects of their experiences of travel with explorers, wanderers, and holiday-makers. From the insightful journals of classical authors to the weekly articles in the travel section of the Sunday newspaper, the literature of travel reflects the rich diversity of man's odysseys, as well as the fantasies and fears, the joys and travails that all travelers face in common.

One chapter in the history of travel has been strangely neglected, however—the ways in which objects have been designed to carry other objects while we travel. *Bon Voyage: Designs for Travel* leads us on a guided tour of the necessities and the luxuries that have accompanied man on his journeys around the world. We are deeply grateful to Louis Vuitton for their sponsorship of this publication and its accompanying exhibition, *Bon Voyage: Designs for Travel*, as well as for making available to us a number of distinguished pieces of luggage from their historical collection. Their cooperation and assistance, along with that of many others, has been essential to the completion of this project.

**Lisa Taylor**
Director

# Dedication

We, the heirs of Louis Vuitton, continue to uphold the traditions which he set in the designing of elegant yet practical accessories for travel. Thus, we were delighted to have been asked to sponsor *Bon Voyage: Designs For Travel* at the Cooper-Hewitt Museum.

As is apparent in so many areas of modern life, we tend to take for granted a host of factors which make possible for most of us a personal convenience and comfort in travel that would never have been imagined by past generations.

In 1854, Louis Vuitton developed his first trunk, which became the ideal accessory for travelers. Therefore, he would be extremely pleased by the charm and worth of an exhibition devoted to design issues which have shaped the equipment for man's continuing journey across the face of the globe. We are especially happy to be able to join with the other lenders to the exhibition and share with them and the Cooper-Hewitt's public this chance to think about the definitions of excellence and the forms of enduring value which emerge from these documents of our past. To all who join us now in this delightful journey, Louis Vuitton wishes Bon Voyage!

**Henry L. Vuitton**
Chairman of the Supervisory Board, Louis Vuitton

**Henry Racamier**
President and Chief Executive Officer, Louis Vuitton

# Introduction

Most people engage in some form of travel at least once in their lives. For some, like the nomadic tribes of Western Asia, travel is a way of life that has endured for millennia. For others, like emigrants, a single voyage can mean the start of a new life. The basic motives for travel have changed little from antiquity to the present. Ancient Romans traveled widely on diplomatic and military missions; medieval Christians made long pilgrimages from Europe to the Holy Land; Renaissance princes moved their courts to various palaces and hunting lodges throughout the year; eighteenth-century gentlemen completed their educations with a "Grand Tour" on the Continent; and Victorian travelers enjoyed train excursions to seaside resorts and indulged in stylish ocean crossings to and from Europe. Twentieth-century travelers are mostly tourists and businessmen, but also include men and women who make scientific expeditions to the most remote regions of the earth and even into outer space.

Whether hiking the Appalachian Trail or riding in a space shuttle, a traveler must carry luggage. Clothing, food, in some instances even shelter, must be taken along if none will be available en route, not to mention money, passports, tickets, maps, guidebooks, and anything else a traveler considers necessary for his journey.

Certain basic criteria of luggage design have remained constant throughout time. Portability and protection have always been foremost: a good traveling case can make even the most fragile items portable. When Princess Pauline Borghese traveled in the early nineteenth century, she carried with her a large mahogany box masterfully fitted with ninety-six items for use

**Noah's Ark**
(detail)
c. 1590
Jan Sadeler (1550–1600),
after Marten de Vos (1531–1603/4)
The Netherlands
Engraving, 23.3 × 30.3
Cooper-Hewitt Museum, New York.
Purchase, Pauline Riggs Noyes Fund,
1953-173-2

**Straw-covered suitcases**
c. 1920s–30s
United States
Wood, straw, leather, metal,
19 × 65 × 36.5 (largest)
Private Collection

**Designs for luggage**
From *Album der neuesten Londner und Pariser Musterzeichnungen für Sattler, Riemer, Läschner und Wagenbauer*
Germany, 1846
Engraving, 33.5 × 25.5
Collection of Louis Vuitton, Paris

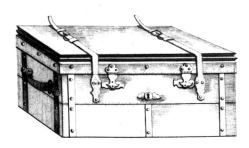

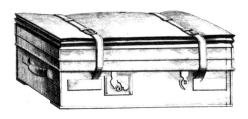

in dressing, eating, writing, and needlework, including cut-crystal bottles and jars, mirrors, silver-gilt tea and coffee services, porcelain plates, and mother-of-pearl-handled manicure tools.

Protection from the elements is also essential. Since ancient times leather has been one of the most widely used materials for carrying cases. Not only is it impervious to wind, rain, and snow, it is also light in weight and tough. Modern-day improvements have come in the form of materials durable enough to withstand even the temperature extremes of travel in outer space. New forms of nylon, dacron, plastics, and fiberglass are now used for traveling cases of all kinds.

The need for protection from highwaymen and thieves has also figured into luggage design. The Roman's *arca ferrata* was a trunk constructed of

**Luggage designs**
c. 1920s–30s
Ernest Deutsch-Dryden (1883–1938)
Germany
Pencil and gouache on paper, 53.6 × 38
Private Collection

The luggage designs included in this
illustration are for a weekend bag,
a shoe case, a vanity case, and a
cabin trunk.

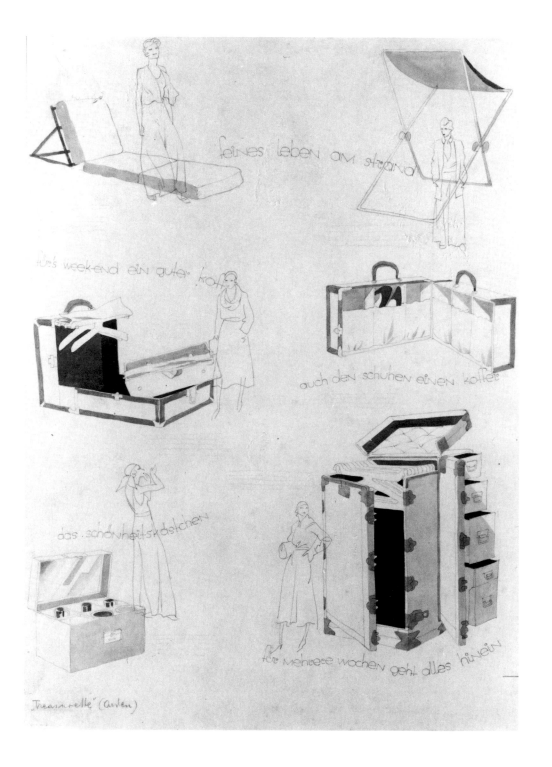

wood reinforced with heavy iron bands. Renaissance princes protected their money and jewels in iron coffers fitted with complicated locking systems. And contemporary businessmen carry high security documents in cases with individualized combination locks.

The whims of fashion have brought about some of the more interesting variations in luggage design and have just as readily caused the demise of others. The collar case, a stiff-sided round box made to hold detachable shirt collars, was an essential part of a gentleman's luggage up until the early part of the twentieth century, at which time collars were fixed onto shirts for good and no longer needed their own cases. Large hats, hoop skirts, and bustles required capacious trunks that eventually followed their contents into obscurity with changes in fashion.

Luggage styles have also changed with developments in transportation technology. One interesting aspect of this change is that while the machines we travel in seem to be growing in size and complexity, our luggage requirements seem to be shrinking. A person traveling by coach in the seventeenth century might have brought along a jumble of large, odd-shaped trunks and bags, whereas a traveler on a jumbo-jet airliner today is induced to carry the smallest, most compact luggage possible.

Anyone traveling on foot keeps his luggage to a minimum. The pilgrim has traditionally traveled with little more than a wide-brimmed hat, a cloak, a staff, a pouch (often hanging from his staff), and a water gourd—creating a silhouette not unlike that of the hobo with his straw hat and his bandana bundle hanging from the stick carried over his shoulder, or that of the hiker with hat, rain poncho, walking stick in hand, and canteen hanging at his side.

Numerous articles of luggage have been designed specifically to be carried on horses, donkeys, elephants, and camels. Cavalry soldiers and cowboys attached leather portmanteaus or bedrolls to the backs of their

**Carriage Design**
From *Journal de Distribution des Fourrages pour l'Ecurie de S. A.sse S.me E.me M.gr le Cardinal de Rohan*
1782–85
Louis René Édouard (1734–1803)
France
Pen and black ink, watercolor on off-white paper, with overlay, 30.6 × 41
Cooper-Hewitt Museum, New York.
Gift of Sarah Cooper Hewitt.
1931–84–34(7)

By using an overlay, the illustrator of Cardinal de Rohan's "stable journal" was able to show this carriage both without its luggage and with the flat case fitted to the roof of the carriage, the two trunks carried over the front and rear wheel axles, and the bags attached to the front pedestal.

**Immigrants from *Prinzess Irene* landing in New York**
early 20th century
Photograph
Courtesy National Park Service, Statue of
Liberty National Monument, New York

saddles and draped saddlebags across the backs of their horses. And for centuries nomadic peoples from Western Asia have loaded their camels with colorful saddlebags, tent bags, and bedding bags made of richly dyed wool, knotted or woven in patterns similar to those of Oriental carpets.

Luggage for horse-drawn coaches often took a specific shape complementary to that part of the vehicle to which it was meant to be attached. Some trunks were made in odd trapezoidal shapes to fit close againt the curving side of the coach, others were arched carefully to match the contours of the roof. Yet others, made to be stacked on the tops of carriages, had domed lids and animal-hide coverings with the hair left on to deflect rain and snow.

The advent of train travel in the nineteenth century inspired significant changes in the kinds of luggage with which people traveled. Dome-topped trunks and odd-shaped cases gave way to large trunks with straight sides that could be stacked in baggage cars. Wooden reinforcing battens and iron and brass corner mounts were added to withstand rough handling. Smaller cases such as carpet bags, leather valises, and shawl straps stayed with train travelers in the passenger cars.

Sea travel has generated its own luggage forms, too. Sailors' sea chests had canted sides for extra stability and looped rope handles that were woven in intricate patterns by off-duty mariners. Oceanliners called for large steamer trunks that were designed to serve as closets or dressing tables or even as writing desks in passengers' state rooms.

Like coaches, early automobiles required luggage that fit the contours of the vehicle. It was not until the 1930s that the word *trunk* referred to the luggage compartment of an automobile rather than to a piece of luggage strapped onto the back bumper. Early automobile luggage trunks were self-contained units, fully detachable, often holding several carefully fitted smaller cases. Wicker picnic sets, leather-covered tool kits, and spare tire cases were also strapped to bumpers and running boards. Short "weekends" and limited space in automobile trunks encouraged the use of smaller valises and suitcases.

Travel in jet airplanes has reinforced the trend towards more compact and lightweight articles of luggage. Shorter traveling time, the assurance of supplies available at destination's end, and the nuisance of checked baggage have also led to a predominance of "carry-on" luggage. Perhaps in a way we have come full circle: the modern air traveler, with trenchcoat, umbrella and overnight case slung over his shoulder, recalls once more the image of the pilgrim, his cloak, staff, and pouch the extent of his necessary luggage.

Many people at Cooper-Hewitt Museum and elsewhere have generously contributed their time and expertise to make *Bon Voyage: Designs for Travel* a reality. Special thanks, however, must be given to David Revere McFadden, Curator of Decorative Arts, for his continued guidance throughout the project. Dorothy Twining Globus, Robin Parkinson, Cordelia Rose, and Steven Langehough all provided expert advice on the planning and installation of the exhibition, and Larry Deemer, Louise Reinhardt, Arabelle Taggart, and Madeline Greenberg also offered their kind assistance.

**Deborah Sampson Shinn**

# Notes on Foreign Travel

## J. G. Links

The armchair traveler (dare one associate that gently-mocked figure with the reader of this volume) is conscious of a watershed as his reading takes him over the pass dividing the sixteenth and seventeenth centuries. The scene from the road has changed, but that has always been changing; now, it seems, the traveler himself is different. He has lost, or is fast losing, his closest companion who gave him warmth as well as mobility: his horse has become a beast of burden, drawing a wheeled vehicle as any ox or ass might do as well, and he has turned from a rider to passenger. But this is not all. The traveler is impelled by a different inner force. His spirit has changed. It is one of the purposes of these notes to enquire what has happened to him.

At once we find ourselves asking who "he" is and meet with difficulties. Is a soldier a traveler, or are those who flee from his sword? Hardly, it seems. Our traveler must go voluntarily if we are to listen to his tales. What then of the traveler who ascends mountains or creeps through potholes? We may listen but can never put ourselves into his shoes. The explorer? Well, yes, so long as he does not take us beyond the bounds of comprehension; we can just take in Cathay, but not Lilliput or Erewhon. The traveling salesman or commuter? What can he tell us that we do not know already? And travel, surely, means foreign travel. There is clearly no room for dogmatism. Each of us knows better than the lexicographer what a traveler is – to us. As with *gentleman* (a word closely associated with later travel), we cannot define the word, but we recognize one when we see him.

Today, as for the past three hundred years, those who make journeys they do not have to make use some such word as *curiosity* to describe their

**Studded trunk**
17th century
France
Leather, wood, iron, 60 × 111 × 58
Collection of Louis Vuitton, Paris

**Egyptian funerary models**
2000 B.C. (Dynasty XI)
Tomb of Meket-Re, Thebes
Painted wood, 27 × 47.5 × 7.2
The Metropolitan Museum of Art,
New York. Museum Excavation
1919–20; Rogers Fund, supplemented
by contribution of Edward S. Harkness

**The Flight, with the Holy Family
at the Left**
Plate 10 from the series
*The Flight into Egypt*
1750–53
Giovanni Domenico Tiepolo
(1727–1804)
Italy
Etching, 18 × 23.7
Cooper-Hewitt Museum, New York.
Gift of Eleanor and Sarah Hewitt,
1931–67–78A

motive. (George Leigh-Mallory was doing this when he gave as his reason for wanting to climb Everest, "Because it is there.") Men were traveling, though, for many centuries before the word, or the idea, existed in that sense. There was no need for it, since scarcely anyone traveled who did not have to do so, whether to perform his duties, improve his lot, or make his peace with distant gods. First among these were those who traveled on official business, ranging from princes and ambassadors to functionaries carrying out their orders. They may have been small in numbers, but it was for them that the roads, and the services that went with the roads, were created and kept up; when, later, they ceased to travel, the roads disintegrated. Merchants, who live by finding goods in one place and buyers in another, soon made the greatest use of these roads, although, in the absence of road or river, the merchant has always found some other way to reach his destination. For the rest, we find those ever-familiar travelers, the touring actor and athlete, well established on the roads from earliest times. Pausanias, who was writing guidebooks based

**Metope relief showing Dacian travelers**
1st century
from Tropaeum Trajani
Adamclissi, Rumania
Stone
Deutsches Archäologisches Institut,
Rome

European roads and modes of transportation changed little from Roman times up to the seventeenth century. Many of the same roads built by Caesar's armies were still in use seventeen centuries later. While most people walked, more fortunate travelers rode on horseback or in simple wagons without springs. Most roads were narrow and full of hazards such as rocks and mud, and progress was often maddeningly slow.

**Illumination**
From *Chroniques et Conquêtes de Charlemagne*, Ms 1067, Folio 149v
15th century
France
Manuscript on vellum
Bibliothèque Royale Albert I<sup>er</sup>, Brussels

on his own travels around A.D. 150, introduces another familiar traveler, the invalid in search of a cure who is willing to go almost anywhere to find it. Epidaurus in southern Greece met the needs, both medical and spiritual, of many of these. The traveling student came later, with the founding of universities or their forerunners.

It did not follow that all those who had to travel disliked the process. The most celebrated of all the earliest recorded travelers, Herodotus, was historian first and geographer only by necessity; yet there is much evidence in his books that he thoroughly enjoyed his many years of travel, observing, enquiring, and measuring wherever he went. (Ptolemy, on the other hand, *was* a geographer, and travelers were relying on his misleading work more than a thousand years after it was written in the second century A.D., even though he seems hardly to have traveled at all.) Then there were the various worthies of such substance that one home was not enough for them. Pliny the Younger, for example, found "enchantment in a change of air and landscape and even in merely journeying around one's properties." An invitation from him to a Roman called Gallus has survived in which he mentions that his villa at Laurentum is only seventeen miles from Rome, "so that it is possible to spend a night there after necessary business is done without having hurried the day's work." Pliny was a rich lawyer who could afford such luxury, and travel for him was far from the travail with which the word was for long synonymous. The best known of all classical travelers' tales, Horace's journey from Rome to Brindisi, began with the need for the diplomat Maecenas to negotiate a difficult mission and his wish to have good company (Virgil was also of the party) on the fifteen-day journey of 370 miles.

During the thousand years between the breakup of the ancient world and the expansion of horizons in the Renaissance, most travelers disappeared from the roads, and indeed many of the roads disappeared, too. Even the

**Trunk**
14th century
France
Wood, iron, leather, 54 × 122 × 44
Collection of Louis Vuitton, Paris

**Saint Christopher**
1511
Albrecht Dürer (1471–1528)
Germany
Woodcut, 21 × 21
Cooper-Hewitt Museum, New York.
Gift of Leo Wallerstein, 1951–37–5

Saint Christopher, patron saint of travelers, carries the infant Christ across the river on his shoulders. Like other sixteenth-century travelers, he bears a staff, a cloak, and a pouch hanging from his belt.

**Saint James Major**
Plate 9 from the series *The Twelve Apostles*
1545
Germany
Engraving, 4.5 × 3.1
Cooper-Hewitt Museum, New York.
Gift of Leo Wallerstein, 1950–131–88

Saint James, patron saint of pilgrims, is shown dressed in pilgrim garb as he walks along the road. Santiago de Compostela in Spain, where he was buried, was an important Christian shrine during the Middle Ages, along with Rome and Jerusalem. Pilgrims traveled great distances from all over Europe to these shrines, staying at hostels and monasteries along the way.

shape of the earth was forgotten, and the sphere that Aristotle had known gave way to a variety of ideas of differing terror. For this the Church was largely responsible, with such influential members as St. Isadore preaching, a thousand years after Aristotle, that the earth was a flat disc. Flat or spherical, the men of business continued to traverse it. In the year 700 the French Bishop Arculf described Alexandria as "the emporium of the whole world, for innumerable people from all parts go there for commerce," and Rabbi Benjamin, from Spain, wrote in 1161 that Bagdad was the metropolis of the Mohammedans; it equaled the Christian Constantinople, where "great stir and bustle prevails from the conflux of many merchants from all parts of the world." Nothing could equal the unparalleled richness of the goods in Constantinople, but there was little the Byzantines were prepared to take in exchange from the eager traders except the spices and cottons of the

**Carrying case**
16th century
Italy
Leather, 15.5 × 14.5
Cooper-Hewitt Museum, New York.
Gift of Samuel P. Avery, 1898–6–4

**Case for drinking bowl**
15th century
Flanders
Leather, 16 × 19.2
Trustees of the British Museum, London

Egyptians and the wool and slaves that the Genoese and Venetians had acquired on their own travels.

The merchants, with a few exceptions, were too busy, or too unlettered, to leave records of their travels, and for early accounts we have to rely on the pilgrims and missionaries who began in about 380 with the Abbess Etheria. She traveled from France to the Holy Land and, in recording her journey, unhappily set a very bad example by telling us more than we want to know about spiritual matters and hardly anything about her travels. For centuries most pilgrims in the West followed her practice, but those traveling in the Arab empire were more communicative.

In the eleventh century the Christian pilgrims to Jerusalem took arms and called themselves crusaders. Some, notably Villehardouin and Robert of Clary, joined the ranks of travel writers with their thrilling stories of the Fourth Crusade. Meanwhile pilgrimages were also undertaken by the infidels against whom the Crusades were directed. Ibn-Jubayr was a Spaniard and a scholar who spent two years from 1183 to 1185 on a pilgrimage to Mecca to atone for an inadvertent religious lapse. In 1325 ibn-Batuta left Tangier for Mecca and continued to travel for twenty-eight years; he was no scholar, and doubts are cast on his accuracy, but he was responsible for one of the greatest of all travel books.

The best-loved books of pilgrimages belong to the following century. Pero Tafur, from Spain, visited all Europe, as well as the Holy Land and Constantinople, from 1435 to 1439 and left an incomparable account of what traveling at that time was like. Santo Brasca, a Milanese, left advice on the thoughts that should fill the pilgrim's head; on a more practical level he also told him what to put in his traveling bags, as we shall see. Almost all the pilgrims passed through Venice, where everything possible was done to entertain them while they awaited the ships that were to take them on their

*Pellegrini*

**Pellegrini (Pilgrims)**
From *Nuova Raccolta di Vari Costumi di Roma e Sue Vicinanze*
1844
Stanislao Morelli
Rome
Hand-colored engraving, 21.5 × 28
Ursus Prints, New York

The traditional costume for pilgrims traveling to Christian shrines was a cloak studded with the cockleshells of Saint James (patron saint of pilgrims), a broad-brimmed hat decorated with shells or pilgrim badges, and a staff or walking stick. Missal boxes, pouches, and flasks were commonly hung from the staff or from loops on the belt, as seen on the pilgrim at center.

**Utensils with cases**
16th and 17th centuries
France and Italy
Leather, silk, mother-of-pearl, steel, silver
10 × 4.5 × 3.4 and 28.2 × 5 × 4
Cooper-Hewitt Museum, New York.
Robert L. Metzenberg Collection,
Gift of Eleanor L. Metzenberg,
1985–103–252,–253

**Coffer**
15th century
France
Wood, iron, 11.5 × 17 × 24
Collection of Louis Vuitton, Paris

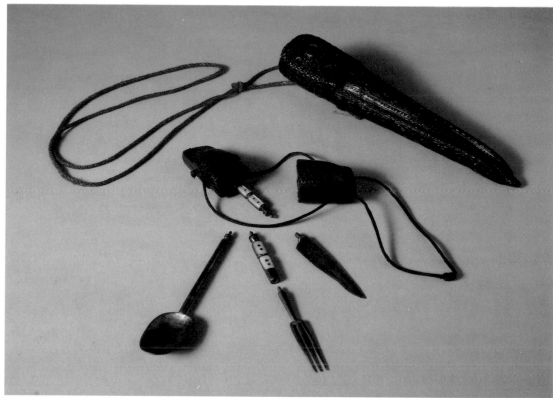

**Illumination**
From *Les Grandes Chroniques de France*, Ms. 1, Folio 1
15th century
France
Manuscript on vellum
Bibliothèque Royale Albert 1er, Brussels

**Coffer**
15th century
Spain
Leather, wood, iron, 31.1 × 63.5 × 40
The Metropolitan Museum of Art,
New York. Fletcher Fund, 1924.

voyage. When William Wey traveled with the Earl of Worcester from Venice to Jerusalem on the so-called Spring Voyage of 1458, he was but one of six pilgrims whose narratives of the journey have survived.

With the coming of the Reformation, Italy lost the profitable flow of pilgrims to the Holy Land but found some compensation in the form of university students. When there were but five universities in England and Scotland, Italy had eighteen, all famous throughout the world of learning. At the end of the sixteenth century an English traveler (Fynes Moryson) noted that foreigners of all nations "still" went to the university of Padua, founded in 1222, "in great numbers."

By this time the world of travel had been transformed by the great explorations. In every direction men were pressing to expand their world, physical as well as intellectual, all of them determined to record their discoveries for posterity. So at least it seems when we contemplate the work of Richard Hakluyt, who first published many of their stories – and even more so when we consider the four hundred volumes of the Hakluyt Society that have been issued in the last 135 years and continue to flow, much to the delight of the kind of traveler with whom these notes opened. Francis Bacon, writing before 1625, noted how strange it was that "in sea voyages, where there is nothing to be seen but sky and sea, men should make diaries; but in land travel, wherein so much is to be observed, for the most part they omit it."

But Bacon was introducing a traveler we have scarcely yet met. "Travel," he wrote, spelling it "travaile," as was normal, "in the younger sort is a part of education; in the elder a part of experience." Scholars might argue the precise seventeenth-century meaning of "experience," but there can be no doubt that the education Bacon had in mind was the education of traveling itself, not academic study: he goes on to explain just how the traveler should

27

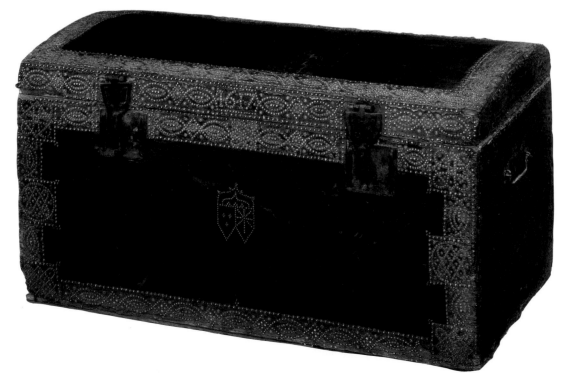

**Studded trunk with cipher of George III**
18th century
Smith and Lucas (makers)
England
Leather, wood, brass,
57.2 × 106.7 × 53.3
Northampton Museums and Art Gallery,
Northampton, England

A variety of large trunks and traveling
cases was used by the courts of Renaissance and baroque Europe as entire
households were moved to various resi-
dences throughout the course of a year.

**Studded trunk with arms of
Marie de Médicis**
1617
France
Leather, wood, brass, iron,
65 × 118 × 61
Collection of Louis Vuitton, Paris

The date incorporated into the decoration of this trunk coincides with the year
that Marie de Médicis was banished
from court by her son Louis XIII.

spend his time, and study plays no part in his program. We have already met travelers who found an agreeable side to journeys they needed to undertake, but the idea of traveling when one did not have to is quite new.

We must not go too far. We have not yet met anyone who traveled simply for pleasure and shall not do so for at least a century. (Even Montaigne, who "took such pleasure in traveling that he hated the very approach to the place where he was to rest," traveled in search of a cure for his stones.) But the word *curiosity* has made its appearance. Mere inquisitiveness about the habits of others was now enough to take one abroad, and "abroad" generally meant France and Italy for the English, perhaps taking in the Netherlands and Germany on the way. Publishers began to feel that the new traveler should offer his experience to others who would welcome details of the practical aspects of traveling — how much it would cost, how long it would take, and, since necessity had not taken them there, what there was to do at their destination. The most informative of the resulting books was that of Fynes Moryson, who traveled through Europe from 1591 to 1595; it was not published, though, until 1617, by which time the better-known Tom Coryat's *Crudities*, recording the author's journey to Venice, mostly on foot, in 1608, had forestalled it.

Bacon's celebrated essay, *On Travel*, was published in 1625. The attitude towards travel had by then changed greatly from the 1590s, when most of his essays were written. *On Travel* might almost have been called *The Grand Tour*, a phrase only just coming into use in 1625, and not to appear in print for another half century. The traveler whom Bacon was addressing was certainly a tourist, although such a word is unrecorded until 1800, by which time the Grand Tour, as we understand it, had completed its two-hundred-year course.

Formal education at foreign universities was becoming unfashionable;

FERDIMAN. MAGALA.

FERDINANDES MAGALANES LVSITANVS *anfractuoso euripo superato, ∞ telluri ad Austrum nomen dedit, eiusque navis omnium prima atque novissima Solis cursum in terris æmulata, terræ totius globum circumijt. An. Sal. ∞.D.XXII.*

4.

instead, the new upper middle classes, from both town and country, sent their sons abroad in the hope that they would come back gentlemen. Bacon specified how this was to be achieved: first, they were to learn the language (but few did); they were to take with them a tutor, or servant, who knew the country (later he was called a governor, later still a bear-leader, and by then his charges were indeed bears in the eyes of many observers); they were not to stay too long in any city, or in the same lodging for long while they were there (good advice); and they were to keep away from their own countrymen and curry favor with those of quality or influence, as well as, if possible, with those of fame ("that he may be able to tell how the life agreeth with the fame"). Courts of justice, fortifications, and antiquities should be observed; comedies were permissible, but only if resorted to by the better sort of persons; so were treasuries of jewels and robes. All these were part of education, and therefore of practical use. There was no question whatever of studying, much less enjoying, the contemporary art of the Renaissance; this would contribute nothing to the making of a gentleman.

Travelers of the traditional kind, of course, continued to go about their business, more to Paris and Amsterdam now, these having become the most influential cities in Europe. Under Elizabeth there had been restrictions on travel for the English; as these were eased Italy became the draw for those who traveled for reasons other than commercial. Some, such as Inigo Jones and John Milton, went with serious purposes of their own; they were far outnumbered by young men who went because their fathers, for the first time, believed it was desirable that their sons should know something of what was going on beyond Dover – and, if wild oats had to be sown, foreign soil was the best place to sow them. It was for such men (and their tutors) that the guidebooks were written. Coryat and Moryson soon had their successors. William Lithgow, who claimed to have walked over 36,000 miles, offered his

**Embroidered trunk**
18th century
Portugal
Leather, silk thread, iron, 43 × 73 × 50
Collection of Louis Vuitton, Paris

**Trunk with marquetry interior**
16th century
The Netherlands or Italy
Leather, iron, various woods,
57 × 119 × 42
Collection of Louis Vuitton, Paris

The rather austere exterior of this trunk
opens to reveal a surprisingly rich interior
of cabinets and drawers covered with
marquetry designs of strapwork and
architectural perspectives.

readers Asia and Africa, as well as Europe; both his book and George Sandys's *Relation of a Journey* sold throughout the seventeenth century. Richard Lassels, who first used the words *grand tour* in print, toured Italy five times, always as "governor" to young men, and in the last edition of his *Compleat Journey*, towards the end of the century, added an essay on the value of travel. Needless to say, there was much repetition on the part of the writers, and most of the readers reacted just as they expected to react.

Yet the impulse to travel out of curiosity grew stronger as the century progressed. Joseph Addison left Dover on the standard tour in 1699, and his subsequent book on his travels opened with the words, "There is certainly no place in the world where a man may travel with greater pleasure and advantage than in Italy." His view of contemporary Italy was a jaundiced one, by and large. However, he did introduce the concept of traveling for pleasure. With Horace Walpole and his friend Thomas Gray, the idea became a reality. They left London in 1739 and almost danced their way to Italy. Both wrote home and, between them, provided an unparalleled picture of two intelligent, high-spirited young men thoroughly enjoying the pleasures of travel and making the best of its pains. They even looked at the scenery. They followed

**Fujiyeda, Post Station**
No. 23 from the series, *Fifty-three Stations of the Tokaido* (Tōkaidō gojūsantsugi)
Edo (present-day Tokyo): Hoeido, 1834
Woodblock print, oban, 24.9 × 36.6
Cooper-Hewitt Museum, New York.
Gift of Mary Rutherford Jay,
1948-134-23

their own tastes, not Bacon's: "Except pictures and statues we are not very fond of sights," wrote Walpole, now in Bologna, and, from Florence, an apology for having done nothing lately but slip out of his domino into bed and out of bed into his domino. "All the morn one makes parties in masque to the shops and coffee-houses, and all the evening to the operas and balls."

They were young – twenty-two and twenty-three – but several years older than the average grand tourist; many were sixteen or younger. These were the men, or boys, whose fathers saw them under the humanizing influence of the Mediterranean, in the company of a cultivated tutor, exchanging ideas with those of similar caste but wider and gentler taste, ultimately returning to take up their responsibilities, more civilized, more gentlemanly, than they themselves had been.

The reality was often different. Lady Mary Wortley Montagu, on whom "inundations of young Englishmen had broken in for the Venice carnival," wrote that they had earned for themselves "the glorious title of Golden Asses all over Italy . . . their whole business abroad being to buy new clothes, in

which they shine in some obscure coffee-house where they are sure of meeting only one another." "Moll Worthless," as Horace Walpole described Lady Mary, perhaps exaggerated, and was herself rather an object of ridicule, but others confirmed her general view.

Others, again, saw it quite differently. The massive volume of material, in the form of published memoirs and guidebooks, unprinted correspondence, and subsequent commentary, is a warning to the judicious student of the dangers of generalization. The eighteenth-century Grand Tour developed from that of the seventeenth century but was quite different, and its own nature changed as the century proceeded. Thousands of people, differing in class, wealth and temperament, were involved, so it could hardly be otherwise.

Many of them no doubt did little to enrich their own minds, but they at least created a heritage of art that England had sadly lacked. Among the thousands of second-rate pictures and faked sculptures that they sent home were many first-rate ones, bought by the more mature tourist who at any rate knew which dealer to buy from. The history of English art collecting in the seventeenth and eighteenth centuries is too complex and erratic for discussion here, but there are worse ways of charting the changing tastes of the nation over that period than by considering the objects with which they filled the crates, trunks, and bales that they landed at Dover on their return.

There were certainly carriages of some sort on the Roman roads, although we can only guess what they looked like: no surviving Roman painting shows one. Horace and his party were "whirled in carriages [*redis*] 24 miles" in 37 B.C., and Pliny the Younger told a guest he would find it slow going if he

**Vargueño and stand**
17th century
Spain
Wood, iron, red velvet,
147 × 105 × 53.5 (vargueño)
Cooper-Hewitt Museum, New York.
Gift of Mr. Harvey Smith,
1968–140–6,–7

The vargueño, a wooden chest with a
drop-front writing surface, a series of
cupboards and drawers, and handles on
the sides, was carried by members of the
Spanish court as they traveled from one
household to another. The traveler either
brought a stand with him or relied on
one at the residence where he was
visiting.

drove to his house near Ostia by carriage but quite easy on horseback. "A traveler in a hurry," advises one of Apuleius's characters, "who goes on horseback rather than sit in a carriage avoids the handicap of luggage, ponderous vehicles with slow wheels, jolting over ruts . . . " and so on. We can even see the tracks made by the wheels of these vehicles at Pompeii, and scholars know, from their names, how many horses drew each kind and how they were harnessed. We can be sure, too, that they were very uncomfortable, and emperors and princes, as well as others who could afford the luxury, were wise to have themselves carried in litters if they did not ride or walk.

Then, unaccountably, wheeled traffic seems almost to have disappeared from the roads until the early 1500s, when Erasmus found a coach of some sort generally available on his journey from Basle to Louvain. Montaigne occasionally hired a coach in 1580 and '81, although he "could not long endure any other transport than horseback." Fynes Moryson had no difficulty in finding a coach, or a seat in one, provided he was in a city, and, in 1618, he wrote that, although very rare in England sixty years earlier, now the streets of London were "almost stopped up with gentlemen's coaches." "But for the most part," he added, "Englishmen, especially on long journeys, ride upon their own horses."

Water transport was obviously preferable to the road if it was available, whatever its disadvantages. When Pero Tafur reached Bologna in 1436, he sold his horses and, he writes, "placed myself and my goods and my people on board a boat and travelled to Ferrara all the way" by the river Reno, which then flowed into the Po – this in spite of the fact that the river froze every night and a waterway had to be broken up for them. (John Evelyn was following the same route two hundred years later, and Arthur Young was complaining of the same journey as late as 1789.) Selling his horses and taking to the water often showed the traveler a useful profit. Felix Fabri, in

**Saddlebag**
late 19th–early 20th century
Persia
Wool, 129.5 × 79
The Textile Museum, Washington, D.C.

1480, rode from Ulm, in Germany, to Treviso, "where many Italians came to our inn who wanted to see our horses and buy them." Moryson strongly advised travelers to follow the same course.

Few travelers seem to have taken to the sea without a storm blowing up, which endangered the lives of all. For the English there was of course no alternative, although it was not exceptional to have to wait a week before crossing the Channel or to take twenty-four hours on the crossing. For centuries there was no real coastal road betwen France and Italy and the traveler normally went by sea from Nice to Genoa. Evelyn was but one of those who "were almost utterly abandoned to despair, our pilot giving us up for gone" on the sea route. Tobias Smollett spent two and a half days being rowed from Nice to Genoa as late as 1764, but if the wind was right fourteen hours under sail was enough. There were dangers even on the Rhine, the principal highway of Europe, despite the disadvantage of constant stops for the payment of duties and tolls to various bishops and princelings. Andrea Badoer's Rhine boat was overturned in a storm while he was on his way to take up the Venetian embassy in London in 1509. We naturally hear little or nothing of the crossings and passages that passed off without event.

For most European travelers the crossing of the Alps provided the greatest adventure of their journey. By Julius Caesar's time there were at least five paved roads over the passes, and lovers of travelers' tales have for long been fascinated by the problem of which of them Hannibal took in 218 B.C. For some the crossing presented no difficulty. Sidonius Apollinaris, on his way from Lyons to Rome in A.D. 467, wrote that he had ascended the Alps easily: "formidable precipices rose on either side but the snow was hollowed into a track and the way thus smoothed for me." Montaigne, in 1581, "crossed Mont Cenis, half-way on horseback, half-way in a litter carried by four men, with another four who relieved them. They carried me on their shoulders. The

**Yomud pouch**
early 19th century
Central Asia
Wool, 34.5 × 33.5
The Textile Museum, Washington, D.C.

**Moving on the Plains**
1873
Cooper-Hewitt Museum, New York.
Kubler Collection

**Parfleche trunk**
late 19th century
Ponca, Oklahoma
Painted buffalo hide, 20.5 × 45 × 35
Museum of The American Indian,
Heye Foundation, New York

Buffalo-hide trunks, called parfleches,
were used by nomadic Plains Indian
tribes to carry their belongings. Strapped
to their horses with other gear, the
parfleches were often painted with geo-
metric designs in bright colors.

Duke of Florence, over whom "they were making a great cry" when Montaigne passed thorough Genoa in 1581. "He had asked permission of the Signoria of Venice to pass through their territory with six hundred horses, to which request they made answer that they would allow him to come with a somewhat smaller number. He put all his people into four hundred carriages and thus brought them all, but he diminished the number of horses."

Travelers, their reasons for travel, and the way they traveled, were always changing. Innkeepers, if the travelers are to be believed, remained the same. They were indolent, rude, dirty and, above all, rapacious. Horace's first stop in 37 B.C. was at Forum Appii, "a town full of extortionate innkeepers" (later, it was St. Paul's last stop on the journey to Rome). The travelers, at any rate in Europe, go on complaining for 1700 years. "Dinner abominable. Foul smells and flies in swarms. Nothing that I could eat, every dish filthy and stinking" (Erasmus on the Rhine in 1518). "Gross meat, sour wine, stinking drink and filthy beds" (Moryson in Germany in 1592). "Almost poisoned by the cookery, half devoured by vermin, and we paid as much as if we had been sumptuously treated" (Tobias Smollett in Italy in 1764). Similiar quotations can be found in almost any book of travel.

The scrupulous reader will have reservations. Good inns make bad travelers' tales and are apt to be overlooked when the time for reminiscence comes. The villainous innkeeper, moreover, seems always to have been in a monopoly position, often as postmaster as well as owner of the only inn in the neighborhood, seldom in a large town where there was competition. Montaigne was greeted outside Florence by well-dressed men "imploring him to choose their inn" and had no complaints of the one he chose (but you had

**Traveling fan**
1788
T. Balister (publisher)
England
Hand-colored print on paper, wooden sticks, 25 high
The Fine Arts Museums of San Francisco.
Gift of Mrs. S. Coursing

to make careful terms "for they will keep you short of wood, candles, linen, or they will fail to supply the hay which you have omitted to specify"). As Smollett noted, "If I am ill used at the post-house in England, I can be accommodated elsewhere," and the publicans vied with each other to give satisfaction, whereas the French postmaster had a monopoly and behaved accordingly.

Nor do we hear the innkeepers' point of view. Roused by ill-tempered travelers at all hours of the night with demands for strange kinds of bedding, and stranger kinds of food, they must have had a great deal to put up with. Few can have been quite as outrageous as Benvenuto Cellini in 1538. Leaving Venice, he spent a night at Chioggia with "capital beds, entirely new and clean." But the landlord had insisted on being paid in advance, and Cellini could not sleep for thinking how he could revenge himself – whether to set fire to the house or cut the throats of four fine horses he had seen in the stable; he settled for cutting four of the beds into ribbons. John Evelyn was a very different kind of man, but, arriving at a small inn in Switzerland on his way home in 1647, he took it for granted that he should "cause one of the hostess's daughters to be removed out of her bed" and go into it while it was still warm. Justice prevailed: the girl had been recovering from smallpox, and Evelyn spent the following month in Geneva, recovering from it himself.

Travelers to the East were more fortunate, particularly if they stayed at one of the great caravanserais (caravan palaces). In these they were accommodated, with their servants to look after them, on an upper floor, the ground floor being given over to their horses (or camels) and their merchandise; a number of these magnificent buildings still exist. When in China, Marco Polo found "numerous fine hostelries for the lodgment of merchants from different parts of the world, and a special host is assigned to each description of people – one for Germans . . . ," and so on.

**Trunk**
17th century
Italy
Leather, wood, iron,
36.8 × 72.4 × 45.8
Northampton Museums and Art Gallery,
Northampton, England

Here, in the segregation of nationalities, lay the clue to satisfaction for both host and guest. Felix Fabri did not have to leave Europe to find it. In Venice in 1480 he stayed at the Flute where the entire household were German, not only the landlord and all the servants, but the dog as well. He received "all Germans with joy but when Italians or men of any country except Germany come into the house he becomes so angry you would think he had gone mad!" A proof, thought Fabri, that Germans and Italians can never agree because each has a hatred of the other rooted in its very nature.

During the second half of the eighteenth century large inns began to be established in the tourist towns, and by the 1760s the word *hotel*, really a large private town house in France, was applied to them for the first time. Dessin's Hotel D'Angleterre in Calais, first mentioned in print in 1768, became famous for the professionalism its owner brought to bear, and he made a fortune out of selling and hiring carriages and changing money, as well as

**Polychromed and studded leather trunk**
late 17th–early 18th century
France
Polychromed leather, wood, brass,
48 × 75 × 42
Collection of Louis Vuitton, Paris

**Deer-hide trunk**
early 19th century
France
Wood, deer-hide, iron, 55 × 110 × 53
Collection of Louis Vuitton, Paris

**Traveling service**
1769–70
Jacques Pierre Marteau (active from
1757) and Nicholas Collier (active
from 1766)
France
Silver-gilt, lacquer, silk,
16.5 × 32.5 × 21.5 (box)
The Metropolitan Museum of Art,
New York. Bequest of Annie C. Kane,
1926

keeping a good and expensive table. Later he got into financial difficulties, but by this time his hotel was such a national asset that he was helped out by the French Government.

The word *restaurant* was first used in 1765, in Paris. There had been forerunners in the form of coffeehouses, of which there were hundreds in both Paris and London by the early 1700s, but these were rather for residents than travelers. Twenty years later, it was said, there were more than a hundred restaurants in Paris, adding much to the amenities of a city where hotels were, by their nature, expensive, and lodgings offering meals, hard to find.

There seems to be general agreement that the least bad inns were in England and the Netherlands; indeed there were good ones to be found in both. It must, perhaps, be remembered that these were the hardest-drinking countries on the normal tourist route. ("Dealer in Spirituous Liquors" was the most frequent sign the German visitor C.P. Moritz saw in London in 1782.) Experienced travelers may therefore wonder whether they just seemed better.

No traveler seems to have approached the gastronomic specialties of his host country with relish. If he had a word of praise for what was put before him, it was because it coincided with what he ate, or drank, at home. The Venetians were astonished at the huge meals of highly-spiced meat served to their German clientele by the Germans who catered at the Fondaco dei Tedeschi (which was opposite the Flute inn): Felix Fabri and his party from Ulm were enraptured by them. Pietro Casola, in Venice at about the same time, "never ate a good fish," although there was plenty of it. Pero Tafur, there in 1438, had been so ill after eating Italian fruit that he warned his readers against it. Twenty years later his words were echoed by William Wey who warned:

**Coffretier-Malletier-Bahutier (Coffer-, Trunk-, and Case-maker)**
From Denis Diderot, *Encyclopédie,* vol. 1, *Recueil de Planches sur les Sciences, les Arts Libéraux et les Arts Méchaniques avec leur explication*
Paris, 1762
Engraving, 30.5 × 22.9
Cooper-Hewitt Museum, New York. Kubler Collection

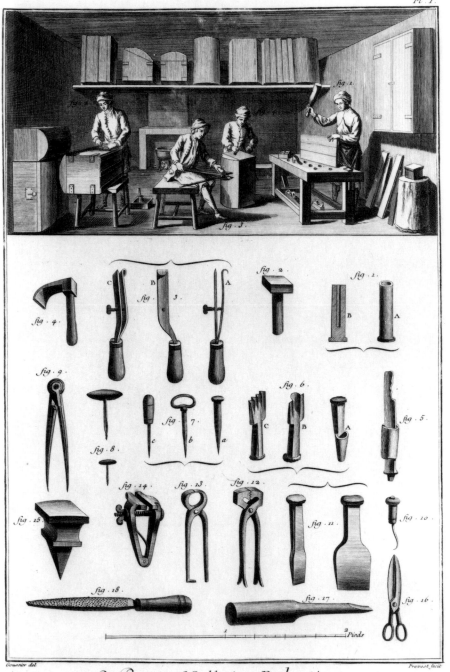

**Case with knives and forks**
18th century
England
Brass, steel, sharkskin, velvet
22 × 12 × 7.5 (case)
Cooper-Hewitt Museum, New York.
Robert L. Metzenberg Collection, Gift of
Eleanor L. Metzenberg. 1985-103-279

"beware of divers fruits for they be not of your complexion and they gender a bloody flux." Coryat died of a flux (probably dysentery) after drinking sack in India in 1617.

The prosperous English ate enormous quantities of butchers' meat and liked it plainly roasted. In other European countries it was necessary to make the best of what was available. "They will eat frogs, guts and all," warned Andrew Boorde of Europeans generally in about 1540, "adders, snails and mushrooms be good meat there," he added. In 1663 John Ray confirmed seeing on sale shellfish, "which we either have not or meddle not with," as well as tortoises and porcupine. Foreigners found these strange creatures more palatable if seasoned with oil, garlic or cheese, but this merely added to the English traveler's suspicions. "Fricassee of frog" summed up the Englishman's view of the foreigner's favorite dish. Nearly everyone commented on the amount of bread the French ate; no one remarked on its superiority to the English kind.

As was to be expected, the traveler to England was astonished by the British appetite. Nicander Nucius, visiting England from Athens in 1546, found his hosts "insatiable of animal food; sottish and unrestrained in their appetites," and fifty years earlier Andrea Trevisano, the Venetian ambassador, considered the English less fastidious than his own countrymen in the choice of game: they ate "what we so much abominate, i.e., crows, rooks and jackdaws." Yet the Italian love of thrushes and other songbirds as food was often lamented.

With their beef the British drank beer. "Few people keep wine in their houses," wrote Trevisano, "but buy it at a tavern." Such was the abundance of ale and beer that they were drunk in great quantities, but "like discreet people, they do not offer them to Italians, unless they should ask for them." Gertrav Hentzner, another German visitor, was not surprised at the preference

**Portfolio**
c. 1725–50
France
Leather, paper, silk, brass,
25.5 × 37.5 × 5.8
Cooper-Hewitt Museum, New York.
Anonymous Gift, 1949-149-1

for ale, although the British "could afford to import the finest wines": the ale was "excellent well tasted, but strong, and soon fuddles."

Almost all travelers, even the beer-swilling English, enjoyed the discovery of unfamiliar, good wine in France and, to a lesser extent, in Italy. There were exceptions, such as James Hume, who managed to find English-type beer in a cabaret in Paris in 1714 – "very acceptable to us who had been reduced for some time to the necessity of drinking nothing but wine." The wine was frequently diluted, in Montaigne's case "generally with a half but sometimes with a third part of water." When he dined with Francesco de'Medici and his wife, "he put in a good deal of water, she hardly any."

Many travelers found water short for the first time in their experience. Horace found to his astonishment, in 37 B.C., that in Ascoli "water, the commonest of all things, is *sold*," and Moryson, sixteen hundred years later, noted that all gentlemen of Venice fetched their water by boats from Fusina, only the poorer sort being content with well-water. Those of the grand tourists who did drink water complained of its quality, Sacheverell Stevens being only one of those who warned (in 1742) that Seine water was responsible for that travelers' bane, the flux.

The moderation of the Italians in their drinking habits surprised many of the English, who regarded them as of an inferior race, and the discovery by travelers of Italian lemonade and ice cream had a deep and lasting effect throughout the world.

Tom Coryat returned from Venice with little but the clothes he had been wearing, and he proudly hung up his boots in his parish church in Somerset. Richard Boyle, 3rd Earl of Burlington, we are asked to believe, arrived at Dover

**Traveling case of Empress Marie-Louise**
1810
Paris
Mahogany, brass, leather, silver, glass,
ivory, mother-of-pearl
Staatlich Schlösser, Gärten und Seen,
Münich

The splendor of life at court followed
many European princes and princesses
on their travels. Some of the most
luxurious travel cases were created in
Paris in the late eighteenth and early
nineteenth centuries. This "nécessaire de
voyage," made for Marie-Louise in the
year of her marriage to Napoleon I,
contains more than one hundred items
for use in washing, dressing, eating,
writing, and needlework.

**Portable sundial**
c. 1685
Butterfield (active 1677–1724)
Paris, France
Silver, shagreen, velvet, 1.4 × 9.4 × 8
Museum of Fine Arts, Boston.
Gift of Mrs. Alfred M. Tozzer

**Portable sundials**
18th and 19th centuries
Germany and China
Brass, steel, wood, leather, paper, silk,
2.6 × 8.6 × 8.9 (largest)
Cooper-Hewitt Museum, New York.
Gift of the estate of Mrs. Lathrop
Colgate Harper, 1957–165–11, –12, –13

Before pocket watches became popular,
a traveler could refer to his pocket
sundial to tell him the time. A compass
and a list of latitudes for major European
cities were needed to make the calcula-
tion and were usually incorporated into
the design of the sundial.

in 1715, after less than a year abroad, with 878 pieces of luggage. What you carried with you depended on who you were and where you were going, not surprisingly.

Perhaps the only surprise is how little the accouterments of travel changed. William Wey's advice, in 1458, to pilgrims about to embark from Venice would not come amiss to the modern camper. He should take with him a feather bed, mattress, two pillows, two pairs of sheets and a small quilt, all of which could be bought for three ducats from a shop in the Piazza San Marco; if he was lucky enough to return from the voyage, the shop would take back everything at half price. He would need both laxatives and restrictives, such as ginger, almonds, rice, figs, and raisins, and, since the food supplied would be at best tasteless, saffron, cloves, and mace to give it interest. "Also take with you," he added, "a little cauldron and a frying pan, dishes, plates, saucers of wood, cups of glass, a grater for bread and such necessaries. Also a bowl for sickness." The traveler must insist on an upper berth for the advantages of air and light. (One hundred and fifty years earlier, ibn-Battuta demanded a cabin to himself, "because of the slave-girls," he reports himself as saying, "for it is my habit never to travel without them"; he had by then completed his pilgrimage to Mecca.) Eggs and poultry, continued William Wey, would be available when the ship touched ports, but the wise traveler should take with him a hen-coop full of live hens and half a bushel of millet seed.

Travelers had always been able to turn to route-books of some kind, with information about posts or, in the case of coastal waters, ports and shipping. With the introduction of printing they could carry their own with them and William Wey's became the model that was more or less followed for centuries (although there is no record that it was itself printed until four hundred years later). As did all guidebooks, Wey's warned the traveler that a passport of

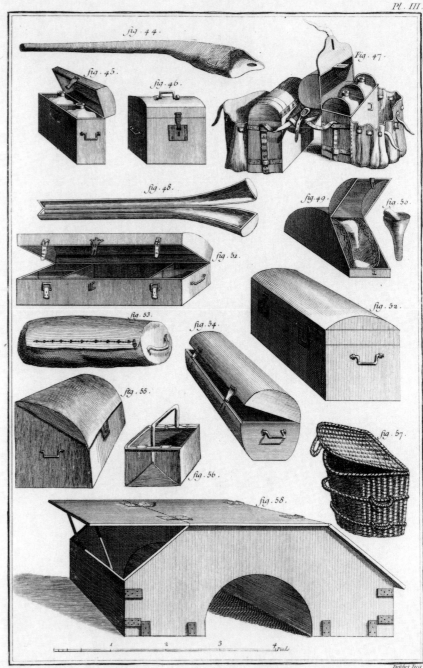

**Coffretier-Malletier-Bahutier**
**(Coffer-, Trunk-, and Case-maker)**
From Denis Diderot, *Encyclopédie,* vol. 1,
*Recueil de Planches sur les Sciences, les*
*Arts Libéraux et les Arts Méchaniques*
*avec leur explication*
Paris, 1762
Engraving, 30.5 × 22.9
Cooper-Hewitt Museum, New York.
Kubler Collection

**Greeley & Morrill trunk label**
c. 1820–40
7.8 × 6.3
Cooper-Hewitt Museum, New York.
Gift of Mrs. Paul G. Darrot, 1969–19–2

Up until the middle of the nineteenth century, most trunks, coffers, and "travelling bags" were made in small shops by leatherworkers who also produced saddles, harnesses, and all kinds of leather equipment. Luggage factories were established as more people traveled and the demand for carrying cases grew. Many of the luggage companies that exist today started out manufacturing large steamer trunks in the late nineteenth century and have adapted their products to the changes in travel and technology throughout the years.

sorts would be needed, in this case a license from the Pope, or a bishop with delegated power to issue one. And as did all later guidebooks, his advised the traveler on the intensely complicated problem of foreign exchange; how, for instance, the Venetian ducat diminished in value the farther away from Venice you went.

Santo Brasca, who began his pilgrimage in Milan in 1480, went a step farther in his advice about money, warning that both gold and silver must be fresh from the Venetian mint, "otherwise the Moors will not accept the coins, even if they be ten grains overweight." He was wise about food, too — a supply of good Lombard cheese and sausages and other salt meats, white biscuits, some loaves of sugar, and several kinds of preserved sweetmeats, but not a great quantity of these last because they go bad; fruit syrup would keep a man alive in great heat, ginger settle his stomach if vomiting. When he goes ashore the traveler should furnish himself with eggs, fowl, bread, sweetmeats, and fruit, and not count what he has paid the captain "because this is a voyage on which the purse must not be kept shut." Indeed, the traveler should carry with him two extra bags, one of them containing two hundred Venetian ducats, one hundred for the voyage and one hundred for illness "or any other circumstances." Pietro Casola, fourteen years later, disclosed what the "other circumstances" might be. Confronted by the Venetian customs officers, he wrote, "my experience proved that it helped matters greatly to shake one of the sacks I had carried with me — I mean that of the money."

Neither was in doubt as to the contents of the extra bag, nor would any traveler, before or since, disagree. It was to be right full of patience.

# Bourgeois Travel: Techniques and Artifacts

**Paul Fussell**

The term *bourgeois*, used here in no pejorative sense, is useful to suggest certain characteristics of the historical period following the Renaissance. The outlines of the Bourgeois Age – sometimes known as the Modern World – are discernible as early as the late seventeenth century. Among its signals are the beginnings of parliamentary government; a growing boldness of intellectual and religious skepticism; a rapidly complicating technology and an incipient industrialism; a heightened egalitarianism, including gestures toward wide public education; and the ascendancy of an ambitious middle class bent on self-improvement in all ways. These forces helped transform the Grand Tour of the seventeenth and eighteenth centuries into the citizens' travel of the nineteenth century and finally the mass tourism of the twentieth.

The instrument of the Grand Tour had been the coach, conspicuously a non- or anti-plebeian vehicle, heavy, tall, exclusive, private, and expensive. Its function as a mechanism of social domination was noted by John Ruskin, who spoke of its "general stateliness of effect" serving for "the abashing of plebeian beholders." (The same effect is aimed at by the modern "limousine.") When Byron left England in 1817, he did so in a bespoke coach costing five hundred pounds – in a day when a hundred pounds was a decent annual income. His coach sported a bed, a plate- and cutlery-chest, and a library. But even private and elegant as it was designed to be, by modern standards coach travel was physically and socially miserable. On the heaviest models, for example, the brakes were so little to be trusted that on steep grades drag-chains had to be deployed out the rear. In the 1760s Edward Gibbon specified the qualifications essential to a traveler: "He should be endowed with an

**Waiting for the Train**
1871–73
James Joseph Jacques Tissot
(1836–1902)
England
Oil on wood panel, 59.37 × 34.27
Dunedin Public Art Gallery, Dunedin,
New Zealand. Purchased from the Funds
of the Thomas Brown Bequest

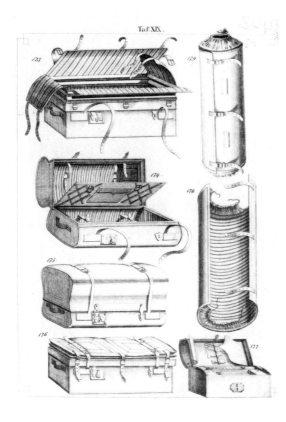

Taf.XIX.

**Designs for luggage**
From *Album der neuesten Londner und
Pariser Musterzeichnungen für Sattler,
Riemer, Läschner und Wagenbauer*
Germany, 1846
Engraving, 33.5 × 25.5
Collection of Louis Vuitton, Paris

Figures 178 and 179 are variations on
the simple portmanteau or bedroll; figures 173 and 176 show a more elaborate
portmanteau with an expandable folding
top; figures 174 and 175 illustrate a
portmanteau with an hourglass shape
and a top compartment accessible by
means of a fitted flap.

active, indefatigable vigor of mind and body, which can . . . support, with a
careless smile, every hardship of the road, the weather, or the inn." And
indeed, the impediments to felicity were appalling: "Bad roads and indifferent
inns," Gibbon notes; and worse, "the continual converse one is obliged to
have with the vilest part of mankind – inn-keepers, post-masters, and custom
house officers." And even that wasn't the worst of it. In Italy south of Naples,
in Spain, Portugal, the Balkans, Greece, and the Near East, brigands and
highwaymen were to be met with. Travelers had to be not only armed but
crack pistol shots, and their coaches were often equipped with cunning false
floors and similar hiding-places for valuables.

The Napoleonic Wars meant that for some years European travel was
restricted or impossible. It revived with a vengeance after the peace, as it does
after all wars, and as usual, with a startling advance in technology – this time,
the steam engine. (After the Great War, it would be the propeller plane,
newly pressed into bourgeois travel service. After the Second World War, it
would be the jet engine.) When rail travel began in 1825, a "train" consisted
of a number of coach bodies mounted on iron wheels and hooked together,
an eloquent emblem of the overnight democratization of the coach. The
origin of railway cars as demeaned coaches is kept alive by the custom,
honored today even by Amtrak, of calling a passenger car a "coach." By the
1860s and '70s, sleeping cars had arrived to add unheard-of comfort to
traveling, and by the 1880s trains no longer had to stop at station restaurants
for meals. They now had dining cars, and even third-class passengers enjoyed
elaborately ostentatious "luxury" in napery, service, and cuisine. What had
happened to travel in two generations was a comfort revolution. Traveling
could now gratify fantasies of social-class ascension, and the hotels to which
the trains carried travelers assisted the fantasy work, named as they were the
Majestic, the Grand, the Excelsior, and the Palace.

**Portmanteau**
c. 1828–38
James Boyd (maker)
Boston, Massachusetts
Leather, metal, cotton twill,
34.3 × 22.2 × 12.7
Old Sturbridge Village, Sturbridge,
Massachusetts

This kind of portmanteau was designed
to be attached to the back of a saddle
and to hold clothing and other personal
gear.

**Doctor's saddlebags**
c. 1850
United States
Leather, mahogany, velvet, glass,
26.7 × 22.9 × 5
Old Sturbridge Village, Sturbridge,
Massachusetts

**Traveling writing kit**
1829
France
Sharkskin, leather, wood, mother-of-
pearl, metal, paper, 6 × 13 × 9
Collection of Louis Vuitton, Paris

The contents of this compact case include a calendar / almanac, inkwell, blot-
ter, pen, nibs, knife, seal, and scissors.

It was the railway that opened opportunities for mass tourism and gave its originator, Thomas Cook, the bright idea of conveying travelers in groups with reduced fares and no anxieties about arrangements. Considering the ultimate association of tourism with such pleasures of the flesh as nudity, rich diet, and copious drinks, it is ironic that tourism began as an adjunct of the temperance movement. Cook was a thirty-three-year-old Baptist temperance zealot, and his first tour, in 1841, carried 570 teetotalers by rail from Leicester to a temperance rally eleven miles away. Soon he was arranging group tours (dry) to the rugged scenery of the Scottish Highlands, and by 1864 he was doing the Continent, strenuously: one of his tours to Paris enrolled 1500 people. If the tourists loved it, some observers were horrified. The novelist Charles Lever recorded his reaction to one of Cook's announcements:

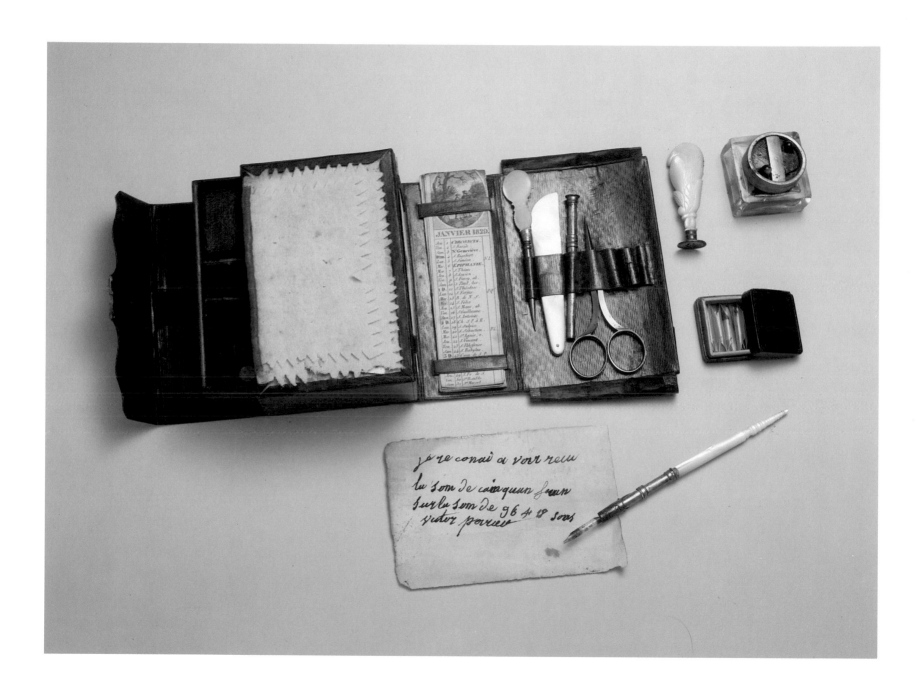

**Le Barbier au Bivouac
(The Camp Barber)**
1876
Jean-Baptiste-Edouard Detaille
(1848–1912)
France
Oil on canvas, 35.5 × 27.5
The Walters Art Gallery, Baltimore

Detaille traveled with the French army
on several different campaigns through
France and Tunisia. Here he records an
early morning scene of a barber with his
clients surrounded by various articles of
camp luggage—trunks, backpacks,
shoulder bags, and mess equipment.

*When I first read the scheme in a newspaper advertisement, I caught at
the hope that the speculation would break down. I imagined that the
characteristic independence of Englishmen would revolt against a plan
that reduces the traveler to the level of his trunk and obliterates every
trace and trait of the individual. I was all wrong.*

He was indeed, and Cook's brand of guided tours flourished as the expansion
of education produced a constantly augmenting supply of curious, if insecure,
aspirants to foreign culture. Contempt for tourism flourished too, until finally
Kingsley Martin stigmatized it as "a disease of the mind, [whose] germ is the
idea that one may learn that which is valuable, or in any way acquire virtue,
by the process of being shown things."

Regardless, a group of sixty satisfied Cook's tourists crossed the Atlantic
in 1866 to be shown the battlefields of the American Civil War, a venture that
a half century of improvements in ocean travel had finally made feasible. Fifty
years earlier transatlantic travel had been a thoroughly miserable affair –
cramped, sick-making, smelly, with terrible food and unremitting discomfort.
The passage often took well over a month. But by the 1860s the *Great
Eastern* was making the crossing in twelve days, and with almost unbelievable
amenity. This iron vessel, almost seven hundred feet long, had six sail-masts,
but was propelled mainly by two immense paddle-wheels, run by coal-
generated steam. Its three thousand passengers unwittingly set the style for
all subsequent sea voyagers by playing deck games, getting their exercise by
loping around the ample deck, enjoying the gas lighting and the hot baths,
attending the nightly musical entertainment in the Grand Saloon, and
consuming excellent food, with plenty of champagne.

Anyone whose experience of long-distance travel is limited to
conveyance by jet will wonder that travel could ever have been comfortable,

**Scholar's traveling kit**
19th century
China
Wood, ivory, stone, brass, pewter, glass
11.5 × 30 × 18.8
The University Museum, The University
of Pennsylvania, Philadelphia

The contents of this traveling kit include
stone palettes, brushes, ink, wax, water
box, magnifying glass, snuff bottle,
scissors, hammer, chisel, tuning fork,
measuring square, candlesticks, mirror,
abacus, and dominoes.

not to say elegant. In addition, it was once an experience humane and social
as well as technological, and there is profound elegiac truth as well as pleasant
light comedy in a bit of dialogue by Noel Coward:

> *"How was your flight?"*
> *"Well, aeronautically it was a great success. Socially, it left quite a bit to
> be desired."*

But if air travel has meant a severe attenuation of one kind of civilized
pleasure, it has opened for millions another kind, the pleasure of visiting on
the run distant exotic sights that the former slow pace of travel put beyond
the reach of all but the very rich. Now anyone with a little cash and a two-
week vacation can flit off to places that seemed out of the question a
generation ago. The travel writer Horace Sutton, who has spent his life
attending to commercial travel and tourism, is aware of the miracle that came
to pass when jet aircraft began to be widely used in the 1960s. "It was a
time," he says,

> *when adventurers of moderate means walked the corridors of far-flung
> museums, . . . bargained in the back alleys of Kowloon, . . . gaped at the
> walled city of Dubrovnik, rowed a boat on the Sea of Galilee, sent home
> postcards from Kyoto — experiences which twenty years before would
> have been too fanciful to have been the stuff of dreams.*

It is just possible that such a miracle is worth all the losses in leisurely
contemplation and deep understanding it has occasioned.

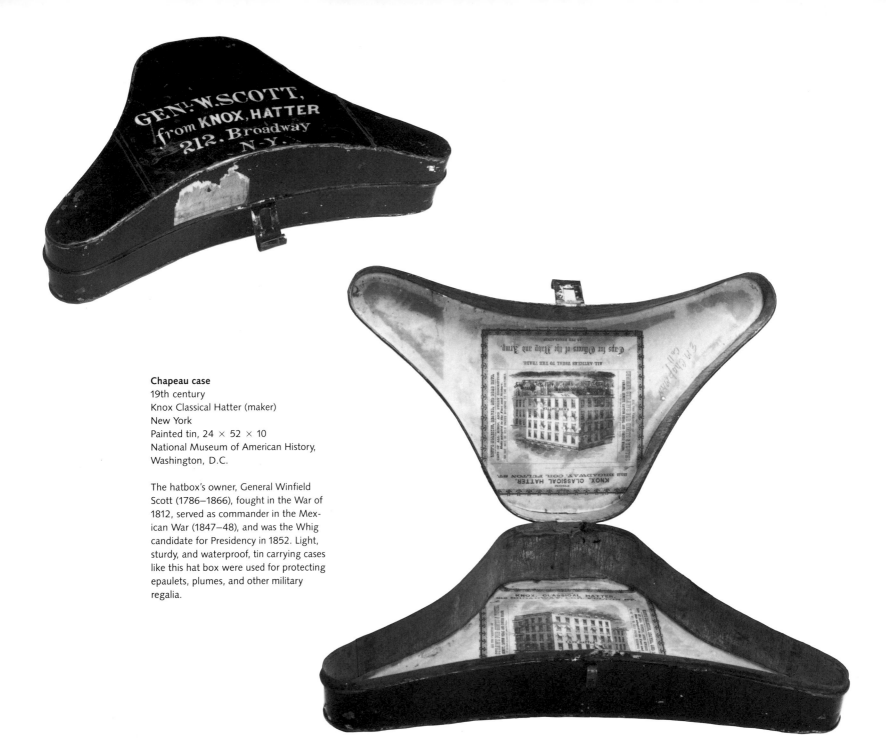

**Chapeau case**
19th century
Knox Classical Hatter (maker)
New York
Painted tin, 24 × 52 × 10
National Museum of American History,
Washington, D.C.

The hatbox's owner, General Winfield
Scott (1786–1866), fought in the War of
1812, served as commander in the Mex-
ican War (1847–48), and was the Whig
candidate for Presidency in 1852. Light,
sturdy, and waterproof, tin carrying cases
like this hat box were used for protecting
epaulets, plumes, and other military
regalia.

**General Winfield Scott**
1851
Cooper-Hewitt Museum, New York.
Kubler Collection

A traveler, whether in 1805 or 1985, is not imaginable without luggage, and from the beginnings of bourgeois travel, luggage has performed a dual function. It has protected its owner's effects, and it has proclaimed – or betrayed – his social status. Whether one consciously hearkens to the middle-class monition, "You Are Known by Your Luggage," both travelers and watchers have always been sensitive to its semiotic powers. If you are content to be regarded as socially low, your suitcase will be made of fiber. If grander, of mock-leather. If grander still, of real leather. If grandest, of alligator, crocodile, Louis Vuitton "LV" canvas, or similar costly stuff. Even entirely severed from its owner, a piece of luggage can testify to his or her identity and circumstances, as Allen Ginsberg suggests about two items "In the Baggage Room at Greyhound":

> — *the Japanese white metal postwar trunk gaudily flowered and headed for Fort Bragg,*

and

> *one Mexican green paper package in purple rope adorned with names for Nogales.*

The geographical, temporal, and social distance is immense between that sort of thing and the elaborately fitted cases made by Louis Vuitton for ladies' and gentlemen's toilet articles of glass and silver and tortoiseshell and ivory; the motorists' luncheon cases with silver plates and cutlery, as well as silver salt and peppers, cups, and corkscrews; and the cases designed for itinerant authors, holding books in shelves together with small typewriters and writing accessories.

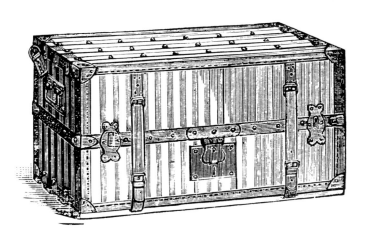

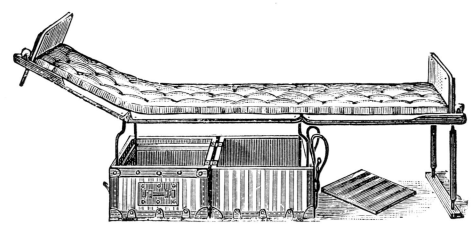

**Traveling bed**
17th century
Sweden
Oak, iron, 35 × 99 × 45 (closed)
Eskilstuna Museums, Eskilstuna, Sweden

**Bed trunk**
1892
Louis Vuitton (manufacturer)
Paris, France
Wood, canvas, brass, iron,
38 × 81 × 38 (closed)
Collection of Louis Vuitton, Paris

A version of this bed trunk, which also
held a hair mattress, two wool blankets,
and four sheets, was used by the French
explorer Savorgnan de Brazza (1852–
1905) during his many expeditions in
Africa.

In the history of luggage since the begin
the evolution, if that's the right word, has bee
from complex to simple, and from elegant to
for this. One is the revolution in dress that ha
last two generations. To go through a collecti
hundred years is to observe that until 1930 or
when appearing in public. Not wearing some
as practically a savage. Travelers to Hawaii app
collars and neckties, wearing Panama hats or
shoes. The loud shirts, "slacks," and canvas sh
astonished them, not to mention the pseudo-
and sandals of a still later day. The motto dom
now conspicuously Dress Down, perhaps mos
the disappearance of men's swim-suit tops in
brazen as female toplessness after the Second

The implications for luggage of this dress
one travels with one bag where formerly seve
necessary for one's formal wardrobe. M. D. Fr
of 1908 spells out the conventions then:

What to Take
*If one goes by an expensive steamship lir*
*hotels, ladies will require an elaborate w*
*evening gowns. Evening dress for gentlen*
*generally the custom in all European citie*
*to keep it constantly at hand.*

**Traveling bed**
17th century
Sweden
Oak, iron, 35 × 99 × 45 (closed)
Eskilstuna Museums, Eskilstuna, Sweden

**Bed trunk**
1892
Louis Vuitton (manufacturer)
Paris, France
Wood, canvas, brass, iron,
38 × 81 × 38 (closed)
Collection of Louis Vuitton, Paris

A version of this bed trunk, which also
held a hair mattress, two wool blankets,
and four sheets, was used by the French
explorer Savorgnan de Brazza (1852–
1905) during his many expeditions in
Africa.

In the history of luggage since the beginning of the nineteenth century, the evolution, if that's the right word, has been from heavy- to lightweight, from complex to simple, and from elegant to plain. There are many reasons for this. One is the revolution in dress that has taken place largely during the last two generations. To go through a collection of photographs of the past hundred years is to observe that until 1930 or so, every man wore a necktie when appearing in public. Not wearing some kind of headgear branded you as practically a savage. Travelers to Hawaii appeared in white suits with stiff collars and neckties, wearing Panama hats or straw boaters and white leather shoes. The loud shirts, "slacks," and canvas shoes of a later day would have astonished them, not to mention the pseudo-workmen's blue-jeans, T-shirts, and sandals of a still later day. The motto dominating then was Dress Up. It is now conspicuously Dress Down, perhaps most notably at the beach, where the disappearance of men's swim-suit tops in the 1930s seemed at first as brazen as female toplessness after the Second World War.

The implications for luggage of this dress revolution are obvious. Now one travels with one bag where formerly several trunks would have been necessary for one's formal wardrobe. M. D. Frazar's *Practical European Guide* of 1908 spells out the conventions then:

What to Take
*If one goes by an expensive steamship line and uses the highest class hotels, ladies will require an elaborate wardrobe, which will include evening gowns. Evening dress for gentlemen [white tie is meant] is so generally the custom in all European cities that it is advisable for a man to keep it constantly at hand.*

**Bandboxes**
c. 1820–30
United States
Printed paper on cardboard,
31 × 39 × 48.5 (largest)
Cooper-Hewitt Museum, New York.
Gift of Mrs. Frederick F. Thompson,
1913–45–13, 1913–45–10.
Gift of Eleanor and Sarah Hewitt,
1917-36-2

Made of stiff cardboard covered with
printed paper, bandboxes were used to
carry clothing and other personal effects.
Their use for travel is often reflected in
the designs of their coverings: the box at
the bottom right shows "Clayton's As-
cent" in a hot air balloon. The box on
the left retains its "Boston, New York,
Philadelphia and Eastern Express" ticket.
The box at the top right is inscribed with
the name of its maker, Putnam and Roff.

**Elegant Dress**
c. 1820–30
England
Brush and gray ink, watercolor, graphite,
30 × 21.4
Cooper-Hewitt Museum, New York.
Purchased in Memory of Katherine
Strong Welman, 1950–97–2

Elegant Dress.

**The Railway Station**
1863
William Powell Frith (1819–1909)
England
Oil on canvas, 116.9 × 256.6
Royal Holloway and Bedford New College, University of London, Egham, Surrey, England

**New Trunk for Hoops**
1857
Cooper-Hewitt Museum, New York.
Kubler Collection

On oceanliners of any pretensions, white tie constituted dinner dress until the 1930s, when it gradually yielded not to the lounge suit but to black tie. Even in second- and third-class hotels and pensions, everyone dressed for dinner. And you needed more than dress clothes. You needed "formal" informal clothes, which had to be correct, like the tweed plus-fours and wool pullovers and caps you needed while strolling the deck in the daytime or playing shuffleboard. These get-ups the shipping company stored at the European port in one of your trunks, which it re-loaded onto the westbound vessel when your European travels were over. This trunk would also contain your masquerade costume, required for hurling yourself with appropriate team spirit into the ship's gala going back. And for touring, you needed formal day-clothes as well, three-piece woolen suits, stout shoes, plenty of white shirts with detachable collars, and generally at least one cane. Women required day dresses for sightseeing, afternoon dresses for tea, or perhaps cocktails, and of course evening dresses for dinner. And lots of beads, handbags, gloves, and scarves, together with hats, hats, hats. Both men and women traveled with hatboxes until well into the twentieth century, and as for shoes — the Louis Vuitton Shoe-Secrétaire of 1926, each of its thirty separate drawers holding a pair of shoes, tells its own story. No wonder, then, that for a steamship passenger twenty pieces of luggage in the hold was considered about normal, with several in the cabin, including, of course, a "steamer trunk," really a portable closet with its own hangers and drawers, providing for at least four changes of clothing daily.

From that down to today's minimal luggage is a long step, and it is astonishing how fast this revolution has occurred, occasioned by the two World Wars, during which the trunk dwindled to the footlocker; by the replacement of ship by air travel; by the invention of easily washable artificial fibers; and by the general proletarianization of life since the Second World

**Hat case**
19th century
France
Leather, metal, 30 × 32 × 26
Collection of Louis Vuitton, Paris


**Home from the Old World—Examination of Baggage by Custom-House Officers on a New York Steam-ship Wharf**
1879
Ivan Pranishnikoff
Cooper-Hewitt Museum, New York.
Kubler Collection

**Carpet bag**
1865–66
Mrs. Rebecca Elsberg (maker)
United States
Wool, glass beads, leather, brass,
41.9 × 43.2 × 14
Museum of the City of New York,
New York. Gift in Memory of Mrs.
Rebecca Elsberg

**Trunk**
mid-19th century
France
Leather, wood, iron, 40 × 84 × 65
Collection of Louis Vuitton, Paris

Made to fit onto the top of a coach, this trunk also provides a cylindrical projection at its center to accommodate one of the large stove-pipe hats popular during the middle of the nineteenth century.

War. If the emblem of the traveler used to be the trunk, or at least the valise, the Gladstone, the tin box, and the hatbox, it is now the backpack. Or even the little stow-under-the-seat-in-front-of-you aircraft bag, in which the skeptical carry one night's needs in case their one piece of checked luggage ends up in Istanbul when they are headed for Paris. The airplane version of this small overnight bag is usually made of plastic and is likely to bear the name not of the traveler but of an airline or a travel agency. (One recalls photographs of the Duke and Duchess of Windsor waiting on some dock beside a pile of twenty or thirty Louis Vuitton trunks, each reading, in beautiful white capital letters with serifs, THE DUKE OF WINDSOR.) Now, what with the disuse of formal dress and extensive wardrobes, a man can travel for weeks with only a carry-on briefcase or attaché case containing a couple of artificial-fiber shirts and extra pairs of artificial-fiber socks and shorts — undershirts have rapidly followed white tie into oblivion — together with a plastic bottle of detergent to wash the whole little plastic wardrobe in.

**Designs for hat boxes**
From *Album der neuesten Londner und Pariser Musterzeichnungen für Sattler, Riemer, Läschner und Wagenbauer*
Germany, 1846
Engraving, 33.5 × 25.5
Collection of Louis Vuitton, Paris

A variety of different shapes of hat cases is illustrated here: figures 149 and 150 show a barrel-shaped box; figures 151, 152, and 153 a cylindrical case with expandable top; and figures 154 and 155 a rectangular-shaped case with several layers of special fittings.

And it would be hard to estimate the blow the tradition of elegance in luggage has suffered from the energetically disrespectful handling of luggage at airports. In fact, a new measure of a very brief moment might be the period of time a former, elegant valise of the classic kind could survive contemporary airport handling undefiled.

In these ways luggage styles over the centuries have accurately expressed both changing social realities and changing modes of transportation. Early trunks, for example, have domed instead of flat tops because they had to be positioned precariously on the roofs of coaches, and the domed top, like a peaked roof, helped get rid of rain and snow. In railway baggage cars and steamship holds, on the other hand, trunks could be stacked: hence the flat lids of later models. From these heavy, earnest attendants of early rail and ship travel to the light fabric carry-alls of air travel, a future archeologist can infer something like the social history of the past two centuries.

In the early nineteenth century, luggage had to be both numerous and copious not just because you carried so many obligatory changes of costume. You also had to carry things either not provided by inns or hotels, or necessitated by flagrant threats to your possessions and person. Mariana Starke's book *Information and Directions for Travelers on the Continent*, published in 1824, advises British readers never to travel without the following, among many other things: sheets, pillows, and blankets, not that these were not sometimes supplied by inns but that their state of cleanliness was likely to appall the genteel. The same with towels, tablecloths, and napkins: the traveler must carry his own. Also a traveling lock for the room door; a mosquito net and a medicine chest, with thermometer. Lamps and

**Violin case**
19th century
United States
Walnut, length 78.6
The Metropolitan Museum of Art,
New York. Purchase, 1980

candles would doubtless be insufficient for reading: one should bring one's own lantern, and not forget matches. Pens, ink, and paper, of course. Inn cutlery would probably be filthy, and dull as well: one must bring one's own knives and forks and spoons, and carving set for roasts and fowl. The inclusion of one's own teapot goes almost without saying. And the Continent not being England, one must also carry "pistols" (note plural), as well as "Essential Oil of Lavender," ten drops of which, "distributed about a bed, will drive away either bugs or fleas." And all this in addition to one's wardrobe. Clearly many trunks would be required.

Writing a year later, the physician Dr. William Kitchener, in his book *Traveler's Oracle,* advises that all these items be packed, and more: not just pistols, but a swordstick as well; a tinderbox for fire-making, and a saw and screwdriver; an umbrella, of course; drawing instruments in their own case, together with sketchbook, pen, and ink. The serious traveler is not to neglect a compass, barometer, and thermometer, nor leave behind opera glasses and telescope. A portable medicine chest is indispensable, and in it Dr. Kitchener

**Advertisement for Louis Vuitton**
1873
Collection of Louis Vuitton, Paris

**"Gris Trianon" trunk**
1858
Louis Vuitton (manufacturer)
Paris, France
Wood, canvas, brass, iron,
59 × 100 × 70
Collection of Louis Vuitton, Paris

The "Gris Trianon," one of Louis Vuitton's early designs made specifically for railway travel, was shown at the Exposition Universelle in Paris in 1867, where it was awarded the Bronze Medal.

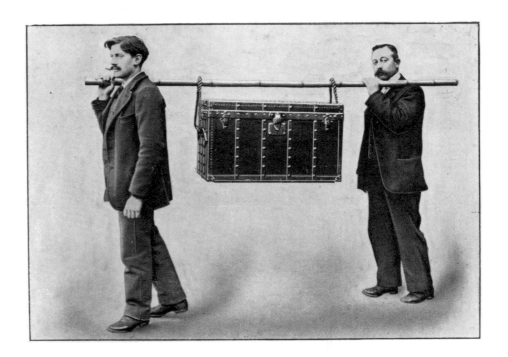

Trunk made for travel in India
1904
Exhibited at the St. Louis World's Fair
Collection of Louis Vuitton, Paris

hopes to find all the standard medicaments, not omitting a good supply of "Dr. Kitchener's Peristaltic Persuader."

If you were headed for any place within the Ottoman Empire, you would need to bring along your own bedstead, together with mattresses and bedding. Otherwise you might find yourself spending nights on damp mud floors fully accessible to vermin. One of Louis Vuitton's most ingenious inventions was his combination trunk and bed, an apparently normal trunk from which, when opened, sprang a bed complete with mattress. For sheer resourcefulness, this item ranks with the light traveling carriage named a tilbury (after its London inventor), which breaks down so that all of it except the wheels fits into three trunks. Louis Vuitton designed these trunks for a lady touring Persia unconvinced that she would find there a vehicle up to her standards.

And even if you took a short rail journey within your own country, you would carry things long since disused, like canes. Most gentlemen equipped

**Sketchbooks: England, New Jersey, Rhode Island, Seashore,**
1865–92
William Trost Richards (1833–1905)
United States
Graphite, pen and black ink, white gouache, 22.1 × 14.4 (largest)
Cooper-Hewitt Museum, New York.
Gift of the National Academy of Design, 1953–179–84, –88, –89

William Trost Richards, an artist who made many plein air studies of the sea in his travels around England and the eastern United States, made this graphite sketch of Lands End in Cornwall in 1892.

themselves with them, both as a sign, like the latter-day necktie, of secure social status and as a handy non-lethal weapon against insolent porters, mad dogs, and the like. (The Grand Tourist a century earlier might have used a sword for this purpose.) On the luggage racks of nineteenth-century trains you might find travelers stashing bird-cages, portable footrests, rugs, portable bathtubs (rubber), bedrolls, water bottles, and of course food baskets. Porters were indispensable then because you carried so much. With the development of modern tourism, and with the expectation that, say, towels will be supplied wherever you stay, the institution of porters has virtually withered away.

What you took along on your travels depended, of course, on the kind of person you were. If you were artistic, you carried not only sketching equipment – the early equivalent of the Kodak – but perhaps also a "Claude Glass." This was an optical device favored by those educated to locate and enjoy the Sublime in scenery. Named after Claude Lorrain (1600-1682), the

**Various Modes of Travelling
in the World**
1855
Cooper-Hewitt Museum, New York.
Kubler Collection

**Collapsible tilbury carriage**
1910
Paris, France
Wood, metal, leather, glass
Collection of Mr. and Mrs. Denizot, Paris

A woman traveling to Persia in 1910,
concerned about the availability of comfortable traveling equipment there, com-
missioned Louis Vuitton to make a set of
special cases that could be used to carry
her collapsible tilbury carriage.

VARIOUS MODES OF TRAVELLING IN THE WORLD.

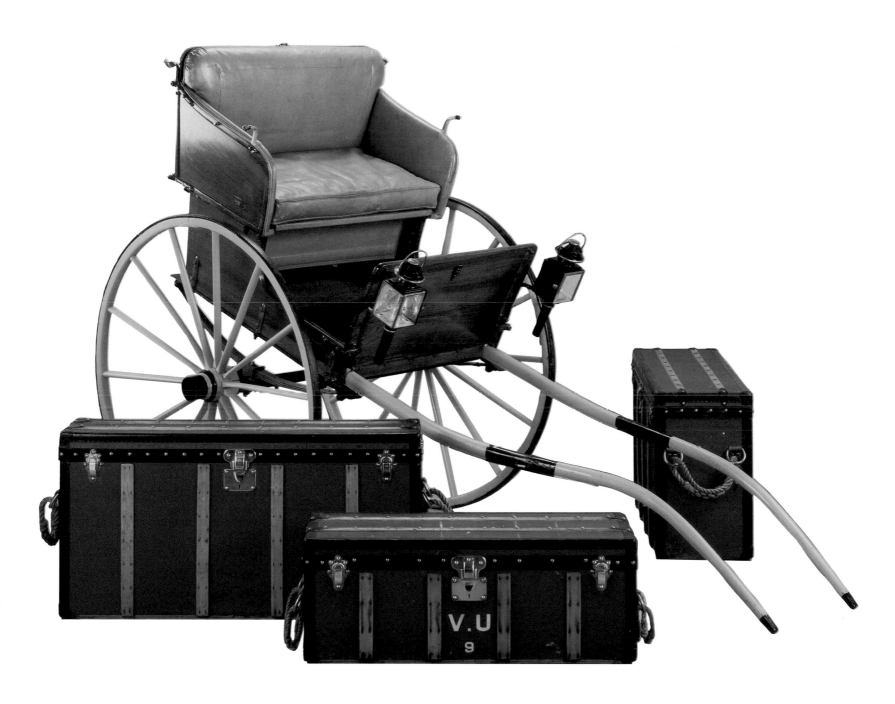

**Trunk with "LV" canvas**
1902 (designed 1896)
Louis Vuitton (manufacturer)
Paris, France
Handwoven canvas, wood, leather,
brass, 56 × 100 × 55
Collection of Louis Vuitton, Paris

**Luggage for a hot-air balloon**
c. 1905
Louis Vuitton (manufacturer)
Paris
Collection of Louis Vuitton, Paris

French landscape painter whose works were thought the most sublime, that is, awe-inspiring, the Claude Glass was a darkened mirror, flat on one side, convex on the other, which gave off a reflection of a scene emphasizing its painterly aspects. When these proved sufficiently sublime – or even picturesque, a less exciting but still sought-after characteristic of scenery – the wielder of the Claude Glass could sketch the view to take home.

It was this vogue of the Sublime that largely made Switzerland a prime tourist goal for a century. As early as 1739 the English poet Thomas Gray was rhapsodizing about the Alps in terms suggesting their future as a magical resource of high-minded tourism. As he wrote his friend Richard West, "Not a precipice, not a torrent, not a cliff but is pregnant with religion and poetry. There are certain scenes that would awe an atheist into belief, without the help of other argument." In addition to serving as world headquarters of the Sublime, Switzerland was also popular both because it seemed to propose a

**Dressing case**
1866
Asprey & Company (manufacturer)
London
Coromandel ebony, brass, silver-gilt,
glass, ivory, 20 × 36 × 27.5
Asprey Limited, New York

The British Government presented this
dressing case to the President of Peru,
José Balta Montero. It represents one of
the most elaborate kinds of traveling
accouterments from a period that did
not shy away from lavish use of precious
materials and ornamentation. The mot-
tled brown coromandel and brass inlaid
case is lined with green velvet and fitted
with ivory-mounted brushes and looking
glasses and with cut-glass jars and bottles covered with flat-chased silver-gilt
lids. Opera glasses, a horn-shaped posy
holder, a scent funnel, and a "secret"
compartment are other special features.

**Elephant-hide trunk**
19th century
Malta
Wood, elephant-hide, brass, iron,
74 × 64 × 60
Collection of Louis Vuitton, Paris

model of enlightened non-monarchical government and because its hotels and restaurants were soon setting a standard for cleanliness and honesty. (César Ritz, whose name became synonymous with excellence in hotels, was a Swiss.)

Thomas Cook early discovered the appeal of Switzerland to bourgeois travelers who wanted to taste the ennobling with a minimum of discomfort, and by 1868 he was sending tour groups of hundreds there. Mountain scenery, both terrifyingly sublime and soothingly picturesque, remained popular throughout the nineteenth century, attracting tourists not just to the Alps but to the Rhine Valley and even to upstate New York. Mountain "views" were the ones most commonly starred as meriting special attention in Baedeker's guidebooks. Italy was not far behind Switzerland as a nineteenth-century attraction, especially its more mountainous parts like the settings of Lakes Como and Garda. Conveyed there by clean and trustworthy railways, you could take long walks, wait for dinner, write postcards depicting hotels, lake steamers, and cheerful, non-insurrectionary peasants, and observe from a distance those awful people from Cincinnati. What with the appeal of Florence and Venice to the artistically sophisticated, Italy became so popular in Victorian times that, as one observer noted, there "almost every other person one sees is a foreigner." Spain probably came next in popularity, despite its more primitive tourist accommodations, because of the romantic charms of Seville and Granada. Relatively uncomfortable also for travelers, but popular nevertheless perhaps because of the asceticism it imposed, was the Holy Land. A nice package could be worked out – and Cook did work it out – combining a tour of the Holy Land with an excursion to Egypt, where Cook had the franchise on the whole fleet of fifteen Nile steamboats.

But bourgeois travel aimed at other sorts of self-improvements than the cultural. Sea-bathing had begun to be thought salubrious as early as 1730,

**Advertisement for Louis Vuitton**
1913
Louis Chalon (b. 1866)
Lithograph
Collection of Louis Vuitton, Paris

**Matchsafes**
c. 1900
England and United States
Silver, 7 × 3.5 × 1 (largest)
Cooper-Hewitt Museum, New York.
Gift of Carol B. Brener and Stephen W.
Brener, 1982–23–930, –1138, –1139,
–1142

**Traveling alarm clock**
c. 1860
Made for Mappin and Webb, London
France
Gilt bronze, metal, glass, leather, velvet,
paper, 15.6 × 11.5 × 11
Cooper-Hewitt Museum, New York.
Gift of Mr. and Mrs. Arthur
Wiesenberger, 1967–66–26

This ornate traveling clock, a type that
was especially popular in the last half of
the nineteenth century, is protected by a
sturdy leather case with one glass side
that can be uncovered in order to read
the face of the clock.

and soon the British beaches of Margate and Scarborough were attracting swarms of holiday-makers. The Prince Regent's Brighton was next, and soon it was discovered that the French Riviera was the place to go not just in winter (it was one of Queen Victoria's favorite retreats) but in summer as well. This meant that sunshine was no longer considered bad for you, and by the end of the nineteenth century what can be called the new heliophily was helping establish on beaches all up and down the Mediterranean the décor and atmosphere of international tourist hedonism. The bathing suit and beach bag would soon replace formal day-clothes and the valise.

Some tourist targets became popular for more mystical reasons. Rome and Lourdes and Fatima attracted Christians replaying the rites of medieval pilgrimage, just as Moslems took the hadj to Mecca and Jews aspired to see Jerusalem. Shakespeare's Stratford became virtually a place of pilgrimage after the Shakespeare Jubilee of 1769, which can be considered one of the first publicity stunts designed to entice tourists. Always popular for its wonders, Egypt became an especially attractive spot in the tourist itinerary after the publicity attending the discovery of Tutankhamen's tomb in 1922. About the same time, for Americans at least, Canada became for some years the place to go: you could not only hunt and fish there. You could get a drink. The same reason helps account for the popularity of Europe (as well as Bermuda) for American travelers from 1920 to 1933. In the 1960s Greece seemed the place everyone wanted to go. One reason was the impact of the film *Never On Sunday.* Another was the immense expansion and publicizing of Aristotle Onassis's Olympic Airlines – for a couple of decades the Greek *sakouli* was the thing for carry-on luggage. Also in the 1960s the vogue of "Eastern religions" promoted Nepal, as well as India, as places to go – and to be seen.

Discovering in the early twentieth century the vast sums earnable through tourist exploitation, countries hastened to establish national tourist

Los Angeles Biltmore

PALACE HOTEL
BRUXELLES

CERNOBBIO
LAC DE COMO
GRAND HOTEL
VILLA D'ESTE
ET REINE D'ANGLETERRE

HOTEL ALFONSO XIII SEVILLA

HOTEL ATLÁNTICO
CADIZ
ESPAÑA

THE BLACK HILLS
TRANSPORTATION CO.

EXCELSIOR HOTEL
NAPLES

YELLOWSTONE PARK
LODGES AND CAMPS

HOTEL HERZLIA
HAIFA & MOUNT CARMEL
מלון הרצליה חיפה
והר הכרמל

**Luggage labels**
20th century
Paper, 12.3 × 14.6 (largest)
Collection of Kenneth Kneitel, New York

**Leaving the Port of London**
1872
Cooper-Hewitt Museum, New York.
Kubler Collection

The luggage porter on the right, wearing
his license badge around his neck,
pockets his fare, while a heated discussion takes place at the left concerning
the luggage of the lady and gentleman
travelers.

**Porter's badge**
1781
London
Lead alloy, 6.7 × 4.7
Museum of London

Porters were available for hire in London up until the twentieth century at stations scattered throughout the city. Badges like this shield-shaped one were worn by the licensed porters as they worked. This one is inscribed "Samuel Shepard, A Freeman, Doctors Commons, 1781," and is stamped on the back with various renewal dates.

offices to publicize the local attractions. Italy was first, in 1919, followed by Holland, Belgium, the Scandinavian countries, Czechoslovakia, Germany, and Japan. Many ingenious schemes arose. In 1936, for example, Yugoslav Railways offered married couples "starting their journey within fourteen days after their wedding . . . a reduction of fifty per cent on the normal fare up till one month after the wedding." The modern tourist trade had found its customers immensely susceptible to hints and leads, and just as *Never On Sunday* performed miracles for the cause of Greek travel – contrast the way travel to neighboring Turkey languished for want of an equivalent film advertising its *louche* delights – so the TV series *The Love Boat* has powerfully reinforced the impulse of middle-class Americans to go on a cruise. Indeed, to survey the vogue of places that have attracted travelers from the beginning of the bourgeois age to the present would be to sketch a virtual cultural and psychological history of the modern world. It would also be to appreciate how central to the modern experience are exotic fantasies and desires – for escape and the foreign, for the novel, the exotic, the non-industrial, the archaic, and the luscious – which can be satisfied, for the moment at least, by travel.

# Design for Travel(ers)

**Ralph Caplan**

Once during a losing battle with insomnia, I got up and plucked from a disorganized bookshelf in a dark room the first volume that felt slim enough to tackle at four in the morning. It turned out to be a book called *Positive Addiction,* a brief exposition of the theory that addiction is perfectly healthy as long as what we are addicted to is healthy. The author himself was high on running, which he endorsed as the addiction of choice. Shopping, he thought, was also good.

My own addiction is more sedentary than running and less expensive than shopping. I am addicted to browsing. Not indiscriminately. I browse for the things I would buy if I were addicted to buying. Books of course, because I am a writer. But also hardware and camera equipment, although I never fix anything and don't take pictures. I just like the stuff, and I like the stores that sell it.

My principal browsing addiction, though, is luggage. If I like hardware, I love luggage. I do travel a lot, but not nearly enough to use all the luggage I covet. In this case, browsing often gives way to purchase. At one time I owned fourteen tote bags, of which I used only two. Now I own four, of which I use one. The secret of browsing is to take it as seriously as you would buying, for the genuine browser's criteria are no less rigorous than those of the most avid consumer.

Luggage, like other packaging, is designed to protect something in transit. The criteria for its design are not esoteric. The luggage I look for, but often don't find, must be sturdy, elegant, and resistant to the grime of cities and the indifference of airline baggage manglers. More important, it must be

**Astronaut Dale A. Gardner**
November, 1984
Courtesy NASA, Johnson Space Center, Houston, Texas

The space suit worn by Astronaut Gardner during extravehicular activities on the Discovery mission can perhaps be regarded as the ultimate form of luggage—made to carry an essential life-sustaining environment.

**John Ross et Son Équipage Gagnent la Mer Polaire**
1876
Cooper-Hewitt Museum, New York.
Kubler Collection

The Scottish explorer John Ross (1777–1856) made two expeditions to the Arctic in search of the Northwest Passage and led another trip to find the Franklin expedition, which had disappeared in 1847. Luggage was carried in sledges pulled by the men.

**Phil Ershler**
October, 1984
North Wall of Mt. Everest, Tibet
Courtesy JanSport and Allied Corporation

Phil Ershler was the first American and the only person on the 1984 expedition to reach the top of Mt. Everest from the north side. Members of the expedition carried equipment for the climb on their backs.

designed to meet the space constraints of various modes of travel as well as my own idiosyncratic requirements.

Luggage design almost always addresses such contradictory needs. The transportation media require uniformity – luggage that will stack efficiently in plane and bus compartments and in car trunks; fit tidily and safely on overhead racks. But the individuality of travelers requires diversity, reflecting differences of purpose, habit, and taste. Yet the interiors of trains and planes are designed as if their cargo consisted of passengers who are all the same size and shape, taking the same kind of journey, carrying the same amount of equipment in identical packages.

Except for such special cases as chartered planes transporting professional basketball teams, passengers are not uniform. Travel is normally done by individual travelers, each with special needs. Students carry books.

**Cars with luggage**
c. 1920s–30s
Collection of Louis Vuitton, Paris

**Car with luggage and skis**
c. 1920s–30s
Ernest Deutsch-Dryden (1883-1938)
Germany
Pencil and gouache on paper,
12.7 × 22.7
Private Collection

**Automobile camper**
c. 1910
Collection of Louis Vuitton, Paris

An early example of an automobile
adapted for recreational camping, this
car, made by Kellner for Louis Vuitton,
featured a reinforced roof that allowed a
sleeping berth on top.

**"Bay West Wash-up Kit"**
c. 1920
Paper 2 × 31 × 14.3
Collection of Stephen Globus, New York

Musicians carry instruments, which, unlike books, come in a wide variety of shapes. (The Grateful Dead buy first-class seats for their instruments). Mothers and fathers carry children (who carry dolls and security blankets) and must therefore carry toys, diapers, and bottles (which must be warmed). Some people carry pets, which must be boxed or bagged. Hunters carry weapons. Photographers carry cameras. So do tourists, who also carry shopping bags full of duty-free liquor. Orthodox Jews carry phylacteries and a battery of special equipment for cooking and eating. Some people carry reading lights. Others bring exercise gear and special pillows and pads for bad backs. Allergy sufferers carry bottles and vials, hobbyists (whoever they are) carry binoculars or X-acto knives. The categories overlap: some students are musicians; some photographers are Orthodox Jews.

What we carry, and what we need to carry it in, varies from person to person, and also varies from time to time with the same person. The traveler's

**Best Trunks on Earth**
From *Sears, Roebuck & Co. Catalogue,*
No. 117, 1908
Reprint edition, Chicago: The Gun
Digest Company, 1969
Courtesy DBI Books, Inc.

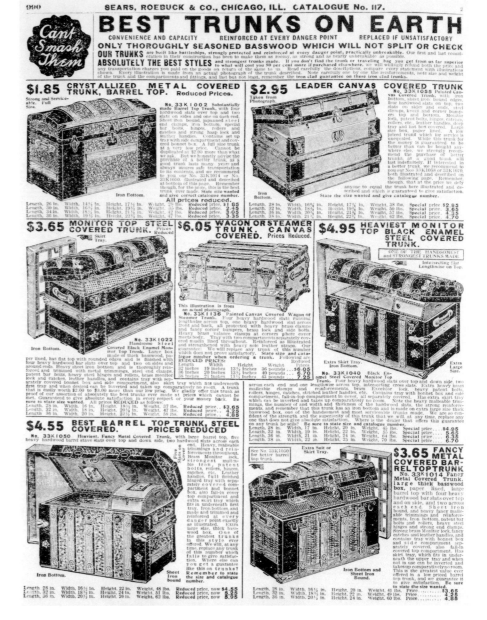

**Les Malles (trunks)**
*La Gazette du Bon Ton*
1914
Collection of Louis Vuitton, Paris

**Packing**
1882
Cooper-Hewitt Museum, New York.
Kubler Collection

age changes, although only in one direction, and the teddy bear is replaced by the mandolin case. Whether hair dryers need to be packed or not depends on hairstyles, which change from year to year, as do lifestyles and workstyles and smokestyles and sleepstyles.

Curiously, as the needs of travelers have become more highly individualized, luggage space has become standardized. Packing for a cruise ship used to be far different from packing for a Pullman car. But passengers boarding the *Love Boat* carry the same kind of luggage they would stow on the red eye from Los Angeles to New York.

**Designs for auto traveling cases**
c. 1920s–30s
Ernest Deutsch-Dryden (1883–1938)
Germany
Pencil and gouache on paper,
32.8 × 30.3
Private Collection

The touring case shown at top incorporates an expandable compartment for maps on one side and on the other a compass and a window for viewing a map scrolled on rollers inside. A folding map section and a compartment outfitted with toiletries accessorize the second case.

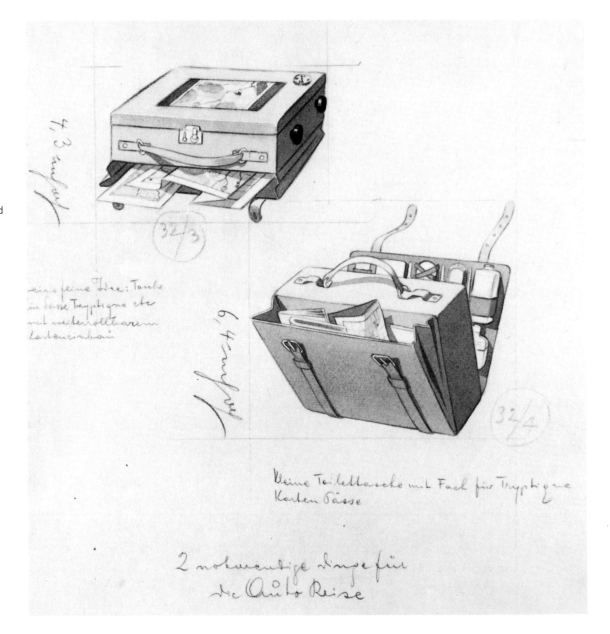

**Sac chauffeur (Chauffeur's trunk)**
c. 1906
Louis Vuitton (manufacturer)
Paris
Canvas, leather, metal
Collection of Louis Vuitton, Paris

Designed to be mounted on the side or the roof of a car, this trunk holds a spare tire and, inside, another smaller trunk suitable for storing hats, overcoats, or chauffeur's equipment. The trunk was made of a waterproof, treated canvas, and when lined with India rubber could also be used as a wash basin.

During the depression a popular jingle went:

*The rich man rides a taxi,*
*The poor man rides a train,*
*The hobo rides the railroad track,*
*But gets there just the same.*

In addition to having no ear for rhyme, the poet who wrote that was no stickler for accuracy either. Rich men and poor men, whatever their vehicle, did not get there just the same, for the former would pack their bags (more often boxes, trunks, and wardrobes) with the assurance that a retinue of servants, Pullman porters, and baggage smashers would help move them. The poor man had no caddy. As for the hobo, the popular cartoon stereotype had him carrying all his belongings in a red farmer's bandana at the end of a stick resting on one shoulder like a rifle during dress parade. I have never seen anyone carry such a device and don't know anyone who has (it seems peculiarly cumbersome to handle while jumping on or off freight trains), but for many it came to signify the romance of the open road.

That romance is inherent in travel of all classes, and this is reflected in design. Dating from the time that a trip abroad was prescribed for everything from anemia to an unhappy love affair, luggage has been invested with a certain designer élan. We want luggage to be dashing, to suggest the adventure of travel, perhaps to remind us of a kind of travel that will never be the same again and never was. (Interestingly, when Hartmann came out a few years ago with a moderately priced line of lightweight nylon soft luggage, they named it "Hobo.") As Betty Cornfeld and Owen Edwards remind us in *Quintessence,* the phenomenally successful Ghurka bags *look* like they are out of Kipling but are in fact out of Norwalk, Connecticut, circa 1976.

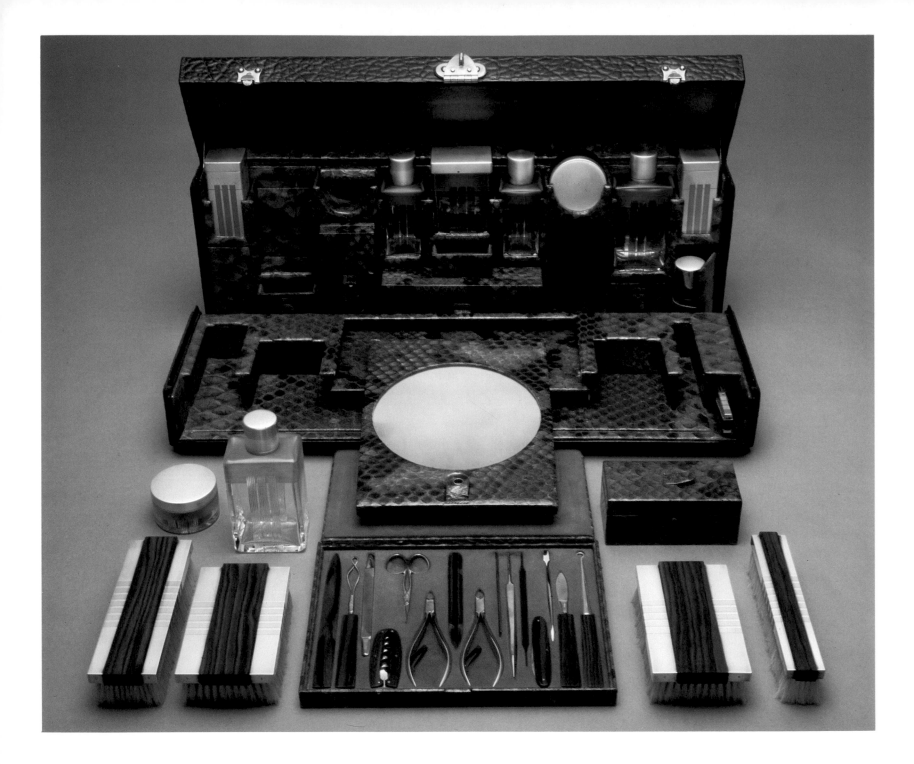

Appearance counts, as it does in other design; and it should. Luggage is your first impression when meeting someone at the station for the first time. Luggage is a means of describing ourselves to the people we care most about impressing, such as prospective in-laws and hotel doormen. At least as much as clothing, luggage indicates taste if not values. Someone with a designer's initials (or the conflicting monograms of several designers) on his luggage is, when he takes his jacket off, likely to reveal a snail or a muskrat embroidered on the breast of his shirt. As a status symbol, luggage has business uses as well as social ones. In *Power*, Michael Korda describes the briefcase as symbol:

> The bulkier the case, the less power its carrier usually has, the lowest power status being that of the salesman's sample case, a big, boxlike piece of luggage in heavy vinyl. Attaché cases that open up to reveal a complete desk, with files and a blotter, are only useful for impressing elderly ladies on airplanes. Elegant, thin attaché cases, however expensive and magnificent, always look like somebody's birthday present to a young executive on the make.

Korda offers some simple criteria for power display:

> All one can say is that a man making less than $50,000 ought to carry an ordinary leather briefcase that opens at the top and has two handles, and that it should be old, battered, and much traveled; a man making more than $50,000 but less than $100,000 should carry a thin leather portfolio, the simpler the better; a man making more than $100,000 should never carry anything . . . .

After the book's publication, Korda reports, "Executives began coming to me and holding their briefcases up for approval like babies to be blessed."

**Paderewski traveling case**
1931
Louis Vuitton (manufacturer)
Paris
Snakeskin, sealskin, silver, brass, glass, macassar ebony, 13 × 57 × 20
Collection of Louis Vuitton, Paris

A descendant of the elaborate eighteenth-century French "nécessaires de voyage," this dressing case, designed for the famous Polish pianist and statesman Ignace Paderewski, is filled with dressing implements made of precious materials carefully fitted into a sturdy, compact, and portable case.

**Traveling case**
c. 1900
Gustav Keller (manufacturer)
Paris, France
Leather, canvas, silver-gilt, glass,
tortoiseshell, metal, 21 × 62 × 39
Musée Carnavalet, Musées de la Ville de
Paris

Retaining its original protective canvas
cover, this leather case is outfitted with
more than sixty pieces, including small
bottles and flasks, mirrors, a writing kit,
sewing kit, manicure set, jewelry kit,
medicine kit, clock, inkwell, and an
alcohol lamp. The case was made for the
Marquis de Dion, an early automobile
enthusiast who held some two hundred
patents for automobile designs.

The business case, however, symbolizes something more than status.
Both a $600 attaché case made of German industrial belting leather with
extended edges and a vinyl envelope that sells for $8.95 in the airport gift
shop symbolize how much of the world's work today is done in the extended
office of hotel rooms, departure lounges, train and plane.

Word-processing technology has meant that entire books, or at least
management reports, could be written in transit; and the sales engineer who,
upon takeoff, produces from its plastic shell a sheaf of specification figures
may be using his luggage to support the best work environment available
to him.

Luggage requires us to carry weights to which we are unaccustomed over
distances we cannot predict. It is not usually designed to help us do this.
Designers today talk freely of "ergonomics." Although ergonomics is only
about ten years old as a marketing ploy, it is over forty years old as a subject

**Advertisement for Asprey luggage**
c. 1920–30
Collection of Asprey & Company,
London

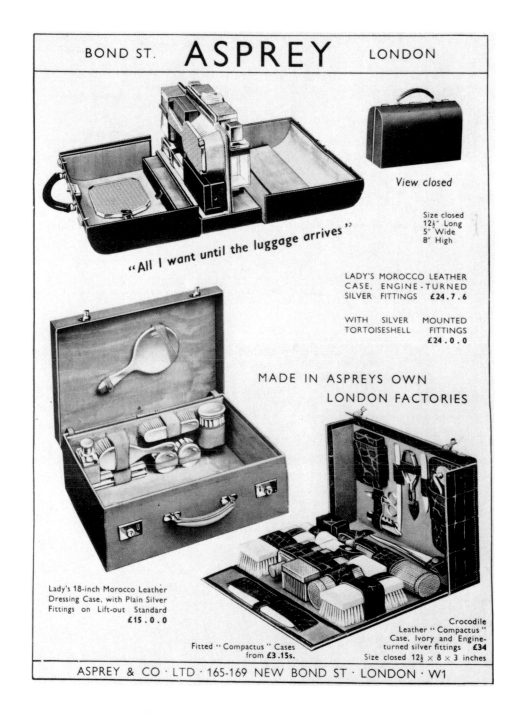

REMARKABLE CONVENIENCE OF THE NEW TRUNK; YOU MAY TURN IT ON END AND DINE IN IT.

**Remarkable Convenience of the New Trunk**
1857
Cooper-Hewitt Museum, New York.
Kubler Collection

for design attention. Hailed as a new science, it is neither a science nor new, but simply an approach to incorporating into the design process as much as designers can find out about the needs, limitations, and capabilities of the person who will use the products. It is strange to think that design would be done any other way. Ergonomics was slow to make its way into consumer goods because the first ergonomists (or human engineers as they were chillingly called in the United States) devoted their skills to areas in which performance was crucial — like flying a bomber. Today we have "ergonomic" chairs and lighting and golf clubs. We even have some ergonomically designed luggage. We deserve more. Luggage is our basic instrument of escape, the collection of artifacts that make it possible to leave house and home temporarily. Birds travel, but leave their belongings in the nest. Pack rats load up, but their purpose is storage not peripateticism. Many species carry food for survival, but we are the only animal that packs for a trip. In the light of that biological specialty, it is surprising how hard it is to decide what to pack and what to pack it in.

Because we need luggage designed to make both decisions easier, it is worth looking at two designs that do: the seabag and the backpack.

The Navy seabag is a good example of luggage that is well designed for one particular purpose. This might be called "dedicated luggage," in the same sense that a word-processing installation is called a dedicated computer: it does one thing well. The seabag holds all the possessions of a sailor or marine. It is in that sense disciplinary: if what you have doesn't fit, then by definition you have too much. It, like the computer, is part of a modular system, for it is ingeniously designed to be the packing module for large groups. Hundreds of seabags can be neatly stored in the hold of a ship, as flour sacks are in a grocery warehouse. Made of canvas too stiff to qualify as soft luggage, the seabag is, like certain cheeses, at least semi-soft.

**Traveling coffee service**
late 19th century
France
Silver, ivory, leather, 10 × 24.6 × 19.4
Cooper-Hewitt Museum, New York.
Gift of Mr. and Mrs. Maxime Hermanos,
1966–6–3

**Wicker picnic basket**
1985
England
Willow, leather, pottery, steel, plastic,
metal, 17.8 × 35.6 × 35.6
Courtesy Abercrombie & Fitch,
Houston, Texas

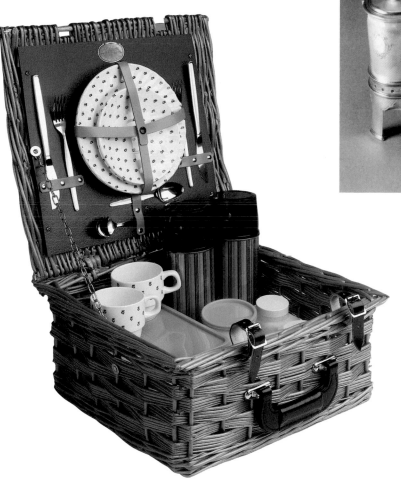

**Traveling iron and folding hangers**
20th century
Metal, leather, wood, 5 × 24.5 × 15.2
(box)
Cooper-Hewitt Museum, New York.
Gift of Mr. and Mrs. Maxime Hermanos,
1969–12–12. Collection of Stephen
Globus, New York.

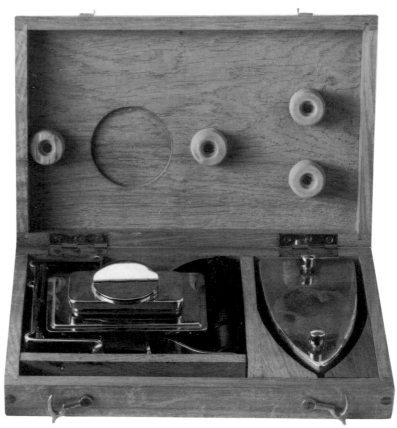
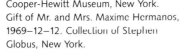

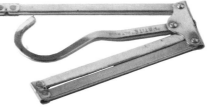

Packing a seabag has been called an art. Actually it is a craft, learnable by almost anyone. The trick is to turn its constraints into opportunities. Because seabags are vertical, everything but the top item is under something else. Because seabags are windowless, only the top item can be seen. To find what you want you have to dig through what you don't want. The secret is to figure out in advance what you won't want and put it where you won't have to confront it again until you do. Living out of a seabag is hard.

Like the windbreaker and the Zippo lighter, the backpack came into popular consumer use after World War II, and, with the help of new materials, technology, and adaptive design, became a modern classic. It is as important and influential as any luggage product has ever been, and quintessentially embodies the design principles and criteria we have been examining.

**Baggage tickets**
20th century
Paper, 12.3 × 17.5 (largest)
Collection of Stephen S. Lash, New York

Attached to the baggage of oceanliner
passengers, these tags indicated which
bags would be needed in the staterooms
and which could be stored in the hold of
the ship during passage.

**Shoe trunk for thirty pairs of shoes**
1926
Louis Vuitton (manufacturer)
Paris
Leather, wood, canvas, brass,
115 × 64 × 40
Collection of Louis Vuitton, Paris

TRAVELLING CLOTHES FOR THE NORTH

**Travelling Clothes for the North**
*Vogue* (English edition)
1924
Collection of Louis Vuitton, Paris

**This is the 1952 Travel Look**
*Ladies' Home Journal*
1952
Cooper-Hewitt Museum, New York.
Picture Library

**Aluminum luggage**
1985
Rimowa (manufacturer)
Cologne, Germany
Aluminum, 77.5 × 52.5 × 21 (largest)
Courtesy HPM Marketing Corp., Cedar
Grove, New Jersey

The backpack's design is specific but adaptable. Designed for foot travel, a backpack must also be used for many other kinds, since few people travel solely (pun equivocally intended) on foot. Unless you live on the Appalachian trail, you can hike it only by first getting to it, a feat not normally accomplished by walking. Also, the more sophisticated modes of travel today involve a great deal of walking. Someone flying from Boston to Minneapolis and changing planes at O'Hare probably walks as far through airport terminals as a combat infantryman did through the steaming jungles of New Guinea. A woman carrying a backpack while fording a stream in Boulder, Colorado, finds the same backpack good for walking through the Denver airport. But a woman carrying an assortment of suitcases on wheels through the Denver airport finds the wheels a burden on any rough surface, or on stairs.

**Garment Bag**
1985
Hartmann Luggage Company (manufacturer)
Lebanon, Tennessee
Nylon, leather, brass, 101.6 × 61 × 10.2
Courtesy Hartmann Luggage Company, Lebanon, Tennessee


**"Diplomat Briefcase"**
1985
Coach Leatherware (manufacturer)
New York
Leather, brass, 41.9 × 28 × 7
Courtesy Coach Leatherware, New York

Ergonomically the backpack is superb, compared to most other luggage. Fifty pounds dangling from an extremity on one side of the body is worse than painful: it can cause serious back and neck problems. A shoulder strap helps, if it is worn across the chest like a Sam Browne belt or supplemented by a hand grip. Although in the fifties industrial designer Tom Lamb did an ergonomically sound study of the human hand in order to design suitcase handles, it was the wrong place to look for a solution. Back and head are the units best situated to assume the weight that the legs ultimately take responsibility for. The backpack is the only luggage incorporating this circumstance into its design, although many derivative products make gestures in that direction.

Backpacks, of course, are not suited to every travel need. They will not keep clothing pressed – some clothing they will not even tolerate – but they are perfect for jeans and T-shirts. Ideally suited to military use, they permit a soldier to carry sixty or more pounds on his back while leaving his hands free for holding weapons and saluting. Since a soldier's clothing is literally uniform,

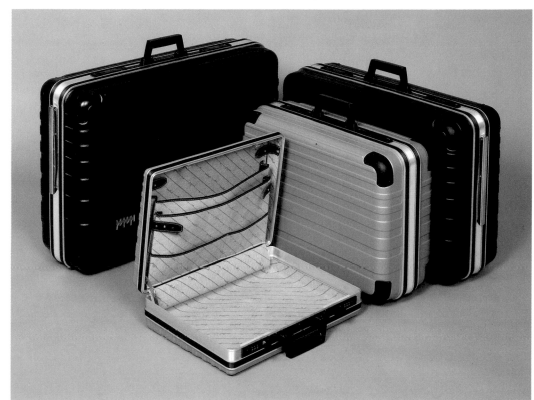

**ABS plastic luggage**
1985
Presikhaf (manufacturer)
The Netherlands
ABS plastic, aluminum, 73.7 × 51 × 23
(largest)
Courtesy L. L. Bean, Inc., Freeport,
Maine

**"Deluxe Seat Bag"**
1985
L. L. Bean, Inc. (manufacturer)
Freeport, Maine
Nylon, cotton, leather, metal,
29.2 × 48.3 × 38.1
Courtesy L. L. Bean, Inc., Freeport,
Maine

Many manufacturers have designed
light-weight, soft-sided cases that can be
stowed under seats or in overhead compartments in airplanes.

each pack holds an essentially identical load. As an item of civilian travel the
backpack came into is own in the sixties, when the rebellion against sack suits
with creased trousers was hottest. Jeans and T-shirts fit very well into a
backpack, like other uniforms.

Because the seabag and the backpack evolved to meet travel needs rather
than marketing needs, there is nothing fallacious in their design. There are
imperfections that need to be designed out of them, but there are no fallacies
consciously designed *into* them, as there are in luggage design that began
with a commercial market.

One such fallacy is omnibus design. My favorite example is the luggage,
advertised in airline magazines, that will hold three suits, a sweater, extra

**First-class passenger amenities**
1985
12.5 × 17.5 and 11 × 16
Courtesy Japan Airlines and Pan American Airways

slacks, raincoat, a briefcase full of work, plus all the extras the traveler may buy while abroad, and still hang in the garment compartment of a plane or fit under the seat. The designer has incorporated into this apparatus a variety of pockets, slots, and pouches to hold sweaters, extra shoes, tennis rackets and what airlines call "smoking materials." It even includes a detachable briefcase. The theory is that the luggage adjusts to any trip, from overnight to six months, and you never have to check anything. The reality is that, if the bag were fully loaded, no flight attendant would admit it to a hanging compartment even if hanging compartments were ample enough to hold it and passengers strong enough to carry it. The physics of traveling decrees that no container can be smaller than its contents. This bag's advertised contents are in themselves too high to put under the seat, too fat to hang in the garment compartment, and too heavy to lift.

Another design error is the fallacy of false proportion, as in the two-suiter with room for a couple of shirts and an extra pair of shoes. Someone carrying two suits must already be wearing something. A two-suiter implies a three-suit trip, which is probably a week's worth of suits. Two shirts and two pairs of socks won't be enough to support the wardrobe unless the traveler intends to do laundry nightly.

A common design mistake is the fallacy of a place for everything. This turns out to mean, in effect, a place for everything specified by the designer who designed the luggage. Some of the most meticulously thought-out suitcases are made difficult to use by the very precision of their design. These are the cases that have built-in toilet kit and pockets for hair dryer, pocket calculator, umbrella, and framed baby pictures. Overdesign of this kind can be worse than no design. Packing, like traveling itself, is personal. At times the best thing a designer can give you is latitude.

Those fallacies all stem from healthy instincts. The fact that travel is

**"The Grip No. 35" camera case**
1985
The Ghurka Collection (manufacturer)
Norwalk, Connecticut
Leather, fabric, brass,
25.4 × 43.2 × 22.9
Courtesy The Ghurka Collection,
New York

simultaneously highly standardized and highly personal makes luggage design especially difficult. One of the thorniest functional problems it poses is that travel today is frequently multi-purpose. A young adventurer going to San Francisco during the Gold Rush probably took everything he owned. A traveling salesman of the same period carried his sample case and a few changes of clothing. But a contemporary airplane passenger may be on his way to a meeting in San Diego, to be followed by a weekend in La Jolla. For the meeting he brings a blue pinstripe suit and black Italian shoes. For La Jolla he wants swimming things, diving gear, a tennis racket, khakis, and loafers.

The solution, as in much modern design, is modularity. But modularity, useful as it is, is not miraculous. For the system to work, there has to *be* a system, a series of components that functionally complement each other. A notable effort in this direction was the TAG luggage designed by Arnold

Wasserman in 1977. An ingenious system of soft but stiff-sided units, TAG was based on the backpack, which is hard to improve upon. Wasserman wasn't trying to improve upon it. He was trying to adapt the ergonomic and convenience factors of the backpack to a more versatile range of luggage. TAG was essentially a backpack with a series of clip-on modules that converted it to a suitbag, a weekend bag, or a portable steamer trunk. Each unit contained snap-up shelves that organized contents as a dresser does, making it possible in theory to live for days without having to unpack. The fallacy was that once you added the snap-on parts, you no longer had the convenience of a backpack. You can't have everything, at least you can't carry it onto a plane. Luggage design is always a matter of trade-offs.

One of Wasserman's objectives was to make the virtues of a backpack accessible to people who wouldn't be caught dead wearing one. Today there are far fewer people in that category than there were in the seventies. Chic backpacks can be purchased at boutiques in magenta leather and worn almost anywhere. Chic aside, these expensive variations of the daypack are useful urban accessories. They leave the hands free for hailing cabs and toting designer shopping bags.

As an urban artifact, luggage has always had secondary uses. It doubles as a stool or a step stool and, where space is at a premium, is used as much for storage as for travel. City people, living in small apartments, use the same suitcases to store summer clothing in winter and winter clothing in summer.

Normally when we speak of travel we think of distance. This is misleading. Urban travelers cover relatively short distances, either on foot or on bikes, subways, and metropolitan buses that will not accommodate much luggage. The design requirements in such cases are special, not just because people carry less than they might for transatlantic voyages but because local journeys have special cargo requirements.

**Harried Businessman gargoyle**
1976
Washington Cathedral
Mount Saint Alban, Washington, D.C.
Limestone, approximately
40 × 36 × 86
Courtesy Washington Cathedral

**Airports**
Poster for the International Design Conference in Aspen
1972
Ivan Chermayeff (b. 1932)
United States
91.5 × 61
Cooper-Hewitt Museum, New York.
1981-29-59

A New York City bicycle messenger, for example, has to carry in the same bag at the same time items ranging in size and character from small parcels to large jiffy bags with books. Some may be fragile, not in the way of fine china, but with the peculiar vulnerability of commerical art mechanicals, photographic negatives, certified checks, engraved invitations. The messenger has to carry them on his person or his bike while weaving through dense and hazardous traffic; and, while delivering one item, must carry all the rest, for the bag cannot be left on the sidewalk. (There is enough risk in leaving the bike.) The Globe Canvas Company in New York, the nation's only manufacturer of messenger bags, produces a large duck bag that is so clearly the industry standard that some delivery firms will hire only messengers who own them.

Messengers are professional short-distance travelers. For most city dwellers short-term travel is not their job but merely one essential component of it. They need briefcases and tote bags to help them get where they are going with what they will need when they get there.

Designers, who have historically put women into shoes not made for walking, have also handicapped them in respect to short-distance, short-term toting. Women's clothing is relatively free of pockets, driving the purse toward portmanteau dimensions. For a long time business women — who went to the same meetings that men did and had therefore the same requirements for papers, file folders, dictating equipment and annual reports — had no briefcases they could call their own. They could buy business cases made for men, which were thought to look incongruous, or carry oversized bags that were the leather or canvas equivalent of shopping bags. Then, we had the briefcase for women. Now we have come full circle. Coach, one of the larger manufacturers of prestige purses, has expanded its line of feminine business cases to include one that is "unisex" — as if there were any other kind.

**Illustration**
1857
Cooper-Hewitt Museum, New York.
Kubler Collection

A BACHELOR AND HIS LUGGAGE.

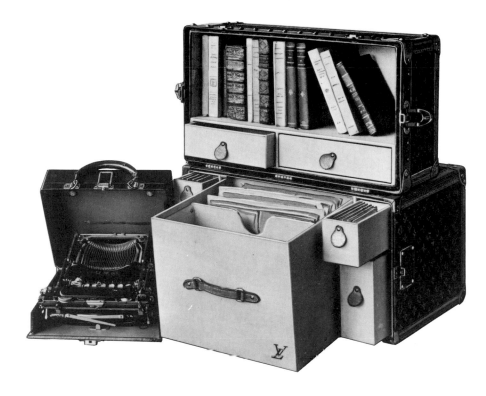

**Library trunk**
1920s
Designed by Gaston Vuitton for his
personal use
Collection of Louis Vuitton, Paris

Feminism, as feminists have always told us, cuts both ways. Men, to be sure, had ample pockets. But only when they were wearing jackets. This, rather than a sense of formality, has kept men in jackets at times when only mad dogs and Englishmen would wear them, for the jacket was the only repository of such appurtenances as eyeglasses, comb, keys, checkbook, appointment book, pens, address book, business cards.

Clearly what every man needed was a purse, just as every woman needed interior jacket pockets. Both were forbidden fashions. The solution to male purse envy came initially not from designers (who are often the last to perceive that there is a problem) but from photographers, who discovered that a camera bag could be used for extra-photographic purposes. Soon camera buffs began loading their cases with personal property never manufactured, or even dreamed of, by Kodak. Many men took up photography solely in order to carry small purchases while in shirt-sleeves.

In the late sixties Bill Blass designed for the Wings Company a canvas

**Desk trunk**
1936
Louis Vuitton (manufacturer)
Paris
Leather, wood, brass, canvas,
94 × 45 × 41
Collection of Louis Vuitton, Paris

Designed for the travels of the conductor
Leopold Stokowski by Gaston Vuitton,
this trunk opens to reveal a desk top,
two shelves for books, two drawers, and
a compartment for storing a typewriter.

"shoulder attaché," which held legal pads, manila folders, books, and had an outside pocket for a newspaper or magazine. The Blass bag was sold mostly in department stores and cost around $30. Totebags today are sold almost anywhere except in banks (where they are given away), and they cost from $9.95 to more than $1,000. You can get them in vinyl, several grades of leather, canvas, fur, and even wood. The variety is dazzling, although I have seen none that surpasses Blass's original, which unfortunately has been unavailable for years.

The traditional materials of the luggage industry — wood, leather, cardboard — are all in use today. To them has been added the lightness and strength of aluminum and, for both hard and soft luggage, various plastics.

Amelia Earhart, as everyone knows, is the name of a distinguished flyer and a brand of luggage. What everyone doesn't know is that Earhart lent more than her name to the luggage. After suggesting to Samuel Orenstein of the Orenstein Truck Company in Newark that the air age required luggage designed for it, she collaborated in developing bent plywood cases and designing fabric covers for them. In design, the people who have the problems tend to be good at setting criteria for solving them.

As early as the thirties there were experiments in rigid plastics for luggage, and by the late forties typewriters and other instruments were carried in molded fiber cases. Nylon suitcases were popular in the fifties because of their lightness. They didn't last long, but were cheap enough to replace often. A slight but genuine innovation was the folding nylon bag designed to be packed flat and to open to become an auxiliary bag when needed on a return trip. In 1973, American Tourister introduced a line of luggage made of uniform molded fiber sides. Designed by John Hauser, this was light, strong, and inexpensive. Fiber shells have since been made stronger, and lighter, and this type of luggage has sustained its popularity in both

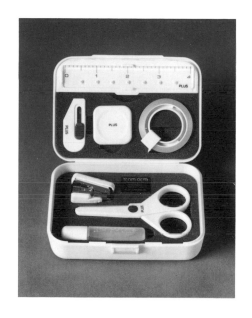

**"Team Demi"**
1985
Plus Corporation (manufacturer)
Japan
Plastic, metal, 3.7 × 12 × 9
Private Collection

The diminutive desk tools in this case are a stapler, water glue, scissors, adhesive tape, measuring tape, blade, and ruler.

suitcases and business cases. It is not the handsomest luggage around, nor the most distinctive, but anyone who has checked an Italian leather case and retrieved it as a scarred and battered mass at the baggage carousel has, however fleetingly, envied the owners of inexpensive hard plastic cases.

Products are designed by designers, but rarely *only* by designers. To a great extent, products can be said to design each other. White sliced bread designed the modern toaster, which in turn designed the Pop Tart. Very few of our automobiles are designed by cities — the London taxi is one of the few exceptions — but our cities are designed largely by the automobile.

This occurs more ambiguously in nature. The egg, as Raymond Loewy pointed out, is an excellent design because it is configured to pass undamaged through the body of a hen. Since the hen is by the same token well designed because it is so appropriately shaped for the laying of eggs, Loewy did nothing to resolve the chicken-and-egg question. In respect to luggage, that question came up recently in a *New York Times* article reporting the airline industry's uncertainty about whether overhead compartments were made larger to accommodate carry-on baggage, or carry-on baggage was made larger because overhead racks would accommodate it.

If the interiors of planes and trains and car trunks contribute to the design of luggage, so do hotels, which are themselves undergoing a design transformation. Because hotels make their money on such peripheral services as banquet facilities and meeting rooms, relatively little innovation has gone into the room itself. Professional hotel management schools, which have proliferated since World War II, still tend to treat design as decoration. A useful guide to thinking about the actual design of travel accommodations is *Work of Art,* which unfortunately happens to be one of Sinclair Lewis's worst novels. No one ought to be allowed to enter the hotel business without reading this clumsy but informative story of Myron Weagle, poet of innkeeping, who strives to create the Perfect Hotel.

**Expandable suitcase**
early 20th century
Louis Vuitton (manufacturer)
Paris, France
Leather, brass, 18 × 60 × 37
Collection of Louis Vuitton, Paris

**Signpost**
Ballyvaughan, County Clare, Ireland
Courtesy Real Ireland Design, Ltd.
Bray, County Wicklow, Ireland

overleaf
**Trunk room**

*He was the inventor, or one of the inventors, of the emergency "overnight kit" for people held too late at the office to get back to the suburbs. It contained cotton pajamas, cheap comb and toothbrush, a small tube of toothpaste; it was given free to sober-looking guests who were benighted, and led several hundred businessmen to making a habit of staying at the Westward. Also, as they were supposed to leave the pajamas behind, to be laundered and used over again, it did not cost as much as it seemed.*

Lewis wrote that in 1934. Fifty years later hotels are beginning to take seriously what are known in the industry as "amenities" – the gratuitous shower caps, shoehorns, sewing kits and vials of shampoo and lotion that now come with all but the meanest hotel accommodations. In 1984 a hotel trade magazine even conducted an "amenities design competition," although the design criteria had to do almost exclusively with packaging.

Many hotels already provide robes and slippers, and some hotels have built-in hair dryers in the bathrooms. That may offer a clue to tomorrow's design for the traveler. Perhaps the biggest changes will not originate in the design of luggage itself but in the ready availability, wherever you go, of things you once had to carry with you. The closer the stuff at your destination matches the stuff at your point of departure, the less luggage you will need. When the match is perfect, you won't need any. And won't need to travel, either, for that matter.

Well, Thoreau distrusted it anyway (" . . . if we stay at home and mind our business, who will want railroads?"), in the conviction that one place was pretty much like another and that the work of man should be to change himself rather than his location. Soon we may not have to move an inch. When that time comes, I won't travel anywhere. I will stay at home and browse in luggage shops.

127